It's Character That Counts

That Counts

Paul C Grassey

Cover: *B24 nose gunner's view*
Photo by Matt Stephan

ISBN: 978-1-932496-95-6
Copyright © 2013 by Paul C. Grassey
All Rights Reserved
Printed by Penman Publishers
Cleveland, Tennessee

*This book is dedicated to my wife Nancy and our
four children: Terry, Bob, Gary, and Marianne;
also my six life-long friends Walt Hays, Bob
Haldane, Don Haldane, Don McCullough, Ed
Van Tassel, and Harry Van Tassel.*

To Dennis + Andrea
I hope you enjoy reading
about "The Greatest
Generation" your Dad were a hero —

Paul Grossy
B-24 Pilot
8th AF

Acknowledgements

Several people told me I should write a book during my later years. What they didn't tell me was how difficult it was to complete the project after the writing was done. It has taken many more people than me to finish this labor of love and these acknowledgements are made not only for the work they have done but for the encouragement they have given me during the last three years.

My son Terry has been a giant of support. Without his superior computer expertise I never could have kept things organized. His encouragement helped to keep me going and he made me stay with my theme;" It's Character That Counts". Terry's patience and work ethic was outstanding as always and it will never be put to a greater test. Thank you very much for a wonderful 67 years.

How can I ever thank Mike Miller enough? One day, during our early morning fitness center visit, a mutual friend asked me how my book was coming along. I told him I had finished writing but it was in need of an editor. Mike said, "I know one." When I asked him for the name, he replied, "Me".

Mike went to work and did the monumental job of two complete edits; after the rewrites, I felt that I had written the book two more times. Talk about patience; I was very fortunate to find another person with "The Patience of Job." Thank you for the professional job you did, my friend.

Speaking of patience—my wife Nancy had to listen to every word I had written each day and give me her opinion. She was a good listener. She would have to be after 54 years listening to me. I love you Nancy! Thanks for a great ride!

To say that Charles Sitrin is a great listener is an oxymoron. He is very kind and drives me to the Mighty Eighth when our work day coincides. But since he is an avid reader and an excellent volunteer, I read to him some of what I had written on the 30 minutes it takes us to get to our destination and, consistently, he has given me good advice. Thank you very much, Charles.

Joan Hays, Elise Haldane, Laurie Van Tassel, and the late Jane Van Tassel , widows of my best friends and Bea Dolan, "Pop" Dolan's daughter-in-law have given me a great deal of support in this labor of love . They have given me pictures and answered any questions I might have, along with plenty of encouragement in this endeavor.

The National Museum of the Mighty Eighth Air Force has given me tremendous support. Our President and CEO, Henry Skipper, actually gave me the name of my book and has encouraged me every step of the way. He also has allowed his staff to give me a hand when I have needed it.

Thank you Jane Grismer, Executive Assistant, and Heather Theis, Director of Educational Programs. Her able assistant, Jaime Hanna, was the first one to suggest that I write this book. Tameka Ford operates and directs our website, www.mightyeighth.org and she did an excellent job setting up pictures for "It's Character that Counts. Thank you one and all.

Contents

Foreword

Bob Carr

Reading this book was a pleasure and honor of the first order. Paul Grassey tells his story (with the help of his son Terry) about his life and the lives of his buddies who helped America win World War II as part of what Tom Brokaw has monikered, the Greatest Generation. For 25 years I have known Paul and he is the truest and bluest of the remaining true, blue American veterans.

Yes, Paul, these men were some of the best of the greatest generation. Yes, Paul, it IS Character That Counts. But you forgot about the leader of this group of leaders and selfless men. You forgot the most effective leader of them all. You forgot Paul Grassey. What could be better than to be memorialized by the great personhood of

Paul Grassey? Paul's "buddies" could not be more honored than by the words in this book. But in my view this book most honors the guy who is saying all of the great things about the buddies who indeed do deserve all of the accolades the author has dispensed!

I am honored to have been asked by Paul to author this forward to this wonderful book. I have known Paul since 1988 when I met him in the waiting room of Colonial Oil in Savannah Georgia. Since that day 25 years ago, Paul and I have been friends and co-workers at Heartland Payment Systems and its predecessor, Credit Card Software Systems. Paul was 65 years old when I met him and I was 42. Paul was at the end of his career and I was in the middle of mine.

When I asked Paul to work for our company, I was surprised that he accepted. He had worked for two great companies – Burroughs and Unisys. Burroughs was contracted by the Department of Defense to build the largest computer of all-time (up until then), Illiac IV, the 256 PE computer designed by the graduate students of the University of Illinois in the late 60s working on grants from the Naval Department. I was lucky enough to be one of those graduate students and I knew how powerful his company was back in those days. I knew that Paul had to have been a stud to have managed New York City for this great American corporation.

But Paul said he was semi-retired and I figured that he might work with us for a bit and hang up his spikes in a short time. But who cared? We had nothing to lose and so Paul came on board. He played a lot of golf and in doing so he made a lot of contacts. Pretty soon he was signing new business for us all around Hilton Head, South Carolina. Paul had quickly become one of the important players in our company. We grew and grew and while Paul did slow down a bit, he was always there and he helped us create the Heartland family.

Paul is the unique kind of person that you instantly enjoy being around. In this book, he talks about his friends and the traits that each of them carried in order to be honored as one of the pillars of "It's Character That Counts". But Paul forgot who was undoubtedly the glue that pulled these great men together to form parts of the many units that saved the world from Adolph Hitler, Joseph Stalin and Hideki Tojo.

Paul Grassey does not give himself the credit he deserves. It doesn't take a long time being around Paul, even at the age of 90, to realize that his personality is magnetic and that he can make you feel like you have known him your entire life. I am not sure that Paul even knows that. I wasn't there, of course, but I strongly suspect that each of the honorees in this book would tell you that Paul Grassey was a central character in their lives and in their careers.

In reading this book, I finally learned the story about Nancy, Paul's second wife. I met Nancy long ago and have always thought she was a very classy lady. When Paul says that the luckiest day of his life was meeting Nancy, he wasn't kidding. Nancy is a wonderful human being and deserves numerous medals including at least one Silver Cross for being married to Paul for all of these years. Nancy was the glue that held the Grassey family together.

She doesn't know this story. Back in the days when I first met Paul, my Mom, Mary Frances Carr, was the company's customer service manager. Mary was the office manager of our company when Paul joined us. My Dad had died and my Mom was a vibrant single woman in her mid-60's. Paul would call the office about all sorts of things with his customers and the processes of getting them started and supported. My Mom never met Paul Grassey except on the telephone. But one day she looked over at me at our small office and told me "I love Paul Grassey" and I think she truly meant it.

What is not to love about this man? Paul was invited to speak at the large gathering of our sales organization, customer service and senior leaders of our company in March 2012. On the closing night of this meeting of almost 2,000 of our closest friends, Paul delivered one of the most emotionally charged speeches ever delivered at our company. He talked about character and he talked about his buddies – the buddies that he brought together by the force of his personality. He talked about why "It's Character That Counts".

He repeated those words which just happen to be at the heart and soul of the company we have both served for these many years. These are words about intellectual honesty and about treating others as you want to be treated. He repeated these words that he memorized so many years ago:

I want to be able as the days go by

Always to look myself straight in the eye.

I don't want to stand with the setting sun

And hate myself for the things I've done.

But I want to go out with my head erect

And I want to deserve all men's respect.

For here in this struggle for fame and wealth

I want to be able to like myself.

Because I know what others may never know

And I see what others may never see;

So whatever happens I want to be

Self-respecting and conscience free.

There wasn't a dry eye in the huge auditorium at the Kentucky International Convention Center after he delivered those words.

Those tears reminded me of a day two decades earlier – a day back in the late 80s in the town of Secretary, Maryland on the Eastern shore. We were a much smaller company then. Folks like Don Lassiter and Tom Schettler were the MVPs in those days. I invited Paul to make the trip up from Savannah. He had told me years before that in the days of his youth, he had spent some time performing in vaudeville shows. He told me that he could still sing some of the old Irish songs. I asked him to sing Danny Boy. He sang it in our small group of 35 or so pre-Heartland people. When he finished, there was not a dry eye in the house that night either. Paul Grassey brought all of us together that night and none of us would soon forget.

Paul Grassey is my hero and has taught me that a person in this era can live a productive, useful and happy life thru his 80s. How wonderful is that? I think it is pretty great. So to this former baseball player, dear husband and father, best friend in the world to his fallen buddies and always cheerful co-worker for 25 "post retirement" years, I say thank you. Thank you for showing us the way to a long and productive life. Thank you for this wonderful book which tells the story of the greatest generation and thank you to his son Terry for helping Paul to write this book and thank you to Nancy for loving Paul for these 53 years through thick and thin. God Bless the Grassey family. Finally, Paul and Terry, thank you for taking the care and the time to tell this story.

—Bob Carr

Introduction

When my wife Nancy and I arrived in Savannah in 1988 and began building our home at "The Landings", I became very involved with The Mighty Eighth Air Force Historical Society. The Mighty Eighth Air Force Museum and the mission that Major General Lew Lyle gave to it have become a very important part of my life.

> *"The mission of The Mighty Eighth Air Force Museum is to preserve for all Americans the stories of courage, character, and patriotism embodied by the men and women of the Eighth Air Force from World War II to the present. The Museum's "Character Counts!" Program fulfills this mission by using the stories and objects of the Eighth Air Force to teach, advocate, and model Six Pillars of Character: Trustworthiness, Respect, Responsibility, Fairness, Caring, and Citizenship. The Museum treasures and teaches these values for the nation's future generations."*

Three of our country's greatest presidents also valued and spoke of the importance of "Character":

George Washington

"Few men have virtue to withstand the highest bidder."

Abraham Lincoln

"Character is like a tree and reputation like its shadow. The shadow is what we think of it; the tree is the real thing."

Dwight Eisenhower

"The qualities of a great man are vision, integrity, courage, understanding, the power of articulation, and profundity of character."

As I approach the age of 90, I realize that many things have happened to me and my life-long friends that could inspire some young people and help them become better citizens-- maybe even help them become more successful in whatever field they choose.

My friends that I grew up with are no longer here to tell their story, and yet they had very successful lives. I believe that it is my duty to tell their stories for them. They played hard, studied hard, worked hard, were successful in school, loved their country, fought for our freedom, loved their families, and were extremely successful in their careers after WWII.

The greatest honor any person can have is to be remembered by future generations for the contributions that he or she has made to help make this planet a better place to live.

Having served in the Eighth Air Force during World War II, I have been given a unique opportunity to give thousands of speeches and presentations about my friends and what they did for their country, their families, their fellow man and their community.

I have written this book so that young people can get a clearer picture not only of what our generation faced but how we responded.

* * * * * * * * * * * * *

Section One -- Beginnings

Here, I introduce you to myself and my friends in the period immediately before our nation's involvement in World War II.

To give you a sense of that period, I involve you in my personal experiences growing up in that tumultuous time. My friends and I played, studied and worked together until the war separated us and we were given our military assignments. Walt Hays, our mentor "Pop" Dolan, and I served in the Eighth Air Force. Bob Haldane was attached to the Eighth, until he was called back to West Point. Don Haldane was in the Naval Air Corps, Don McCullough became a Marine, and Ed and Harry Van Tassel served in the Ninth Air Force.

If you graduated from high school from 1935 to 1942, you were involved in WWII.

Section Two -- Pillars of Character.

In this section, I interrupt my largely chronological story to give you more details about my friends.

As mentioned, I have become involved with the Mighty Eighth Museum in a youth educational program called Character Counts! That program, developed by the Josephson Institute of Ethics, breaks down character into six "Pillars."

I believe that the lives of these men illustrate the six pillars of character counts perfectly. The fact of the matter is, they each could have fit all six. To emphasize the importance of each character trait, I chose to select one of my friends as an example for each character pillar. The following six chapters let you see the consistent presence of these traits throughout their lives.

Character is essential to success in life and it is never too early or too late to learn and develop. In a book I read, *How Children Succeed,* there is a quote that perfectly describes this:

"Character is more important than intellect."

Section Three -- In The Army Air Corps

Here, we return to my personal story and my experiences in the Army Air Corps. In order to win the silver wings of a pilot, there were many steps we had to take. Though our training was shortened by the demands of war, it took well over a year before we saw the cockpit of an actual bomber. Each step had its challenges and the opportunity for serious accident or washout.

Once training was completed, we were ready to prepare ourselves for combat and this is where we met the B24. I tell about those early days of learning to fly this bomber -- which would be my home for the next year. Then we move on to England with a truly dangerous trip across the North Atlantic and to my Eighth Air force Base in Bungay, England.

You will learn how we prepared for a mission and what to expect from takeoff through the forming area. Then along the route to the target, where we met our fighter escorts and where we could expect to meet enemy fighters and, after "bombs away", the route back to England.

I will take you on a couple unforgettable missions for my crew and you will learn about my friend Ed Beebe, an American hero and his plane, "Pin-up Girl". Then I share a few brief comments on the end of combat and my military service.

Section Four -- The Next Steps

I will tell you how important a college education is and how important the "GI Bill" was in restoring the United States of America after this devastating War.

Character is important in business too and I introduce a few men throughout my working career who have had a great influence on me. At critical times they have given me opportunities to make a comeback, have helped me reach my goals, or have been an inspiration for me to reach for that elusive next rung of the ladder.

Finally, I discuss The National Museum of The Mighty Eighth Air Force. I explain how it has allowed me to stay active into the 90's and how successful its Character Counts! program has been for its community.

Beginnings

In this section you will meet me, Paul Grassey, and six of my friends from high school days. Graduating in 1941 and 1942 in New Jersey, we faced a world in turmoil and a nation in the process of gearing up for war.

We all came from different backgrounds and wound up in different places in our lives but we shared a common sense of purpose at that crucial time for our nation.

All joined in the Allied effort. We each contributed in our own way. Some contributed well beyond the actual war. This was not an exceptional group. Men like these could be found throughout the country. But, taken in perspective, they are a group that accomplished exceptional things. There are lessons to be learned from following their stories.

CHAPTER 1

Duty Calls

This story revolves around seven young men who graduated from Ridgewood High School, New Jersey, in 1941-42. These seven had a role model with an unusual military history, Mr. Bill Dolan, a 50-year-old successful businessman and the stepfather of two of the boys.

The young men, age 18, played sports together; attended classes together, and were great friends: Don McCullough, twins Harry Van Tassel and Ed Van Tassel, Don Haldane and his cousin Bob Haldane, Walt Hays, and Paul Grassey. These were the kind of young people you might find on every corner of every town. By the spring of 1942, they had one goal in mind: To put their personal goals of college, sports, or professional careers aside and decide "what branch of military service to join so that we could best serve our country." The United States was at war.

Speaking in London on June 16, 1941, British Prime Minister Sir Winston Churchill made the point entitled *The Spell of Duty*.

"The destiny of mankind is not decided by material computations. When great causes are on the move in the world, stirring all men's souls, drawing them from their firesides, casting aside comfort, wealth and the pursuit of happiness in response to impulses at once awe-striking and irresistible, we learn that we are spirits, not animals, and that something greater is going on in space and time, which, whether we like it or not, spells duty."

I remember my graduation day, June, 1941, as if it were yesterday. War was raging in Europe and the Japanese were causing havoc in the Pacific. Sitting at our graduation ceremony, we had no idea what effect those dark clouds of war would have on our lives but we were thinking about it.

My father's career was in the textile industry and he worked for a time in Havana, Cuba. We returned to the States so I could attend Bergen Junior College while also working night shifts at Wright Aeronautical. Harry and Ed Van Tassel were among my closest friends and worked at a local mill while attending night classes with me. Bill Dolan had two biological sons and was known by the twins as "Pop." I had an older brother who also worked at Wright Aeronautical and who loved to fly. Henry often took me up in a Piper Cub to teach me how to fly. We were at Caldwell, N. J. airport on December 7, 1941, when we learned that our country had been attacked by Japanese forces. Our lives would never the same.

Henry shortly thereafter became a Navy ensign flight instructor at Memphis Air Station. Our friends were getting into uniforms of different branches of the service. I liked the Army Air Corps. I longed for the day that I would be able to wear those silver pilot's wings.

Don McCullough had already joined the Marines and was on the aircraft carrier U.S.S. Hornet when Jimmy Doolittle's B-25 unit took off on their historic mission to bomb Tokyo. Newspaper headlines screamed "U.S. Bombs Tokyo" following that raid—an inspiration to our whole nation.

Decision Time

One Sunday afternoon in the spring of 1942, the remaining six of us gathered at the Dolan home to discuss our upcoming enlistments while enjoying some of Mrs. Dolan's delicious cooking. Pop Dolan, a very confident, well-groomed gentleman, walked into the room. Almost in unison we said "Mr. Dolan, do you think that we ought to enlist?" He replied, "I can't make that decision for you, but I want to show you guys some things." We had known very little of his past, but he returned to the room with pictures of himself from World War I. He had served as a pilot in the Lafayette Escadrille with Eddie Rickenbacker, Carl "Tooey" Spaatz, and other early flyers.

Pop Dolan had gone through the intense French training course at Issoudun, undergoing their unusual but effective methods. We were impressed with his tales.

One week later we all were re-convened in the large sunroom for further discussions when Dolan walked in wearing his Air Corps officer's uniform with Captain's bars on each shoulder and his pilot's Silver Wings. He had re-activated his officer's commission during the week. He said, "I'm leaving for duty on Tuesday. You guys will have to make up your own minds." That motivation was all we needed. Bill Dolan was the first recruit of the 8th Air Force's 384th Bombardment Group.

The story of what happened to the six young men who followed Colonel Dolan into the service of his country centers around one concept: duty to country.

You will learn much more about their experiences during and after the war later but they quickly became part of the massive American mobilization.

Don Haldane earned his Navy Wings of Gold and was commissioned an Ensign. He was killed while on a training mission in July, 1944.

Bob Haldane, Don's cousin, had a distinguished 40-year career in the U.S. Army, graduating from West Point and retiring as a Lt. General. During his career he served in Germany, Korea and Vietnam.

Walt Hayes flew combat missions as a tail gunner with the 8th Air Force's 95th Bomb Group, was shot down over Germany, and ended the war as a prisoner in a German stalag.

Pop Dolan's stepsons, twins Ed and Harry Van Tassel, both achieved the rank of Captain, serving with the Ninth Air Force Troop Carrier Command in France after the invasion.*

---

* Pop Dolan's two sons, Bill and Walt Dolan, also served in the Air Force; flying the Berlin Airlift postwar.

I was fortunate to become a B-24 heavy bomber pilot after completing primary, basic and advanced training at Air Corps training bases in the southern United States. I was assigned to the 446th Bomb Group, 8th Air Force, in Bungay, England. I flew my missions with them during the war.

We put it all on the line because we knew The Price of Freedom!

The six young men who sat in Pop Dolan's living room that day in 1942, influenced by his example, performed admirably as did so many of America's young servicemen during the war. Their lives were changed forever as they became part of the wartime Allied forces of freedom that changed the course of history.

Most of us had returned from our military service by early December 1945, so Don McCullough put together a Christmas party at his grandmother's house in Ridgewood. All these men had seen combat during the war and all of them graduated from Ridgewood

High School between 1938 and 1942. All of them still had to finish college before starting their careers and fortunately would have the GI Bill of Rights to carry them through. This picture becomes even more significant when you understand what these men accomplished upon graduation from college:

Chairman of the Board of AT&T; President of Stone and Webster, Newspaper Publisher; Superior Court Judge; Comptroller of AT&T; District Manager Large Computer Systems; star half-back at Cornell University; football star at the University of Texas who got into the oil business and married the daughter of Glen McCarthy, an oil tycoon who owned the Shamrock Hotel in Houston.

I honestly believe that the GI Bill did more to help almost 2,000,000 GIs get our country back on a peacetime footing than anything else could have accomplished.

CHAPTER 2

Growing Up and Meeting My Life Long Friends

I was born in Glens Falls NY. July 27, 1923. I'm Paul Charles Grassey. My mother's maiden name was Bertha Brandt; she was born in Paterson N.J. in 1888. Her parents had emigrated from Germany. My father was born in Paterson N.J. in 1890. His parents had emigrated from Italy, coming here on an arduous journey in a sailing ship and having no resources upon arriving at Ellis Island, in New York. I had an older brother Henry who was born October 1, 1917, in Paterson.

My father was a textile worker who actually started working in a dye house when he was eleven years old, because his father has passed away and the family needed his income. He had completed only six years of school when he began work. My mother completed eight years of school when she began working in her father's candy store in Paterson. The name Grassey was originally spelled Grassi but was changed by my grandparents who felt that it had the wrong connotation in Italian. We moved to Glen Rock, NJ when I was six months old because my father had been promoted to a supervisor in a Paterson textile company.

Our house in Glen Rock was at 690 Doremus Avenue, last house on the right and right next to a very large wooded area. My grammar school was two blocks up the street. A few years later it was named The Richard E. Byrd School after the famous Artic explorer Admiral Byrd. Another great landmark, a block farther up the street, was the famous huge rock of Glen Rock. Another quarter of a mile up our street was "Doremus Oval" where the Glen Rock AC Baseball Club played big time semi-pro baseball.

To name a few notables who played there: Johnny "Double No Hit" Van DerMeer, Cincinnati Reds; George Sisler, Cleveland Indians; Larry Doby, Cleveland Indians—the first African American to play in the American League. It was the same team I played on 17 years later but I certainly wasn't in their league. However, my friends and I spent many days, weeks, and years there playing baseball and football.

I loved sports, mostly football and baseball. Our grammar school and junior high school didn't have a gym. In fact, I never saw one until I got to high school. The first Christmas presents I can remember were football pants, shoulder pads, cleats, helmet, and a green Notre Dame jersey. Notre Dame was my favorite college team and I dreamed of the day when I might attend the University. After World War II, I was accepted at Notre Dame, to start in March of 1946, but decided to go to Lafayette and play baseball.

Glen Rock was a fine town to grow up in. The population was about four thousand and our neighbor was Ridgewood, where we would attend high school. One of my first life-long friends was a year behind me in elementary school. Walt Hays was a tough little guy and we loved to play football and baseball. Our fathers also loved to hunt and fish. In fact, when we were about twelve years old, they both belonged to a gun club in Radburn, NJ. There we learned how to shoot skeet and became very good at it. We both could shoot twelve-gauge shotguns and would compete with the older men who belonged to the club.

In those days, we had junior high school, seventh through ninth grades, and that is where we met Bob Haldane. A fun loving guy, Bob was very intelligent and loved sports, not too great at them but never gave up trying. Years later he proved to be the toughest of the tough. Walt and Bob were the only children in their families and my brother Henry was six years older than I. I became a catcher because the only way Henry and his friends would let me play baseball with them was to let me catch. I was the only one who would do it with no equipment. My family finally got me a mask and a catcher's mitt.

My favorite relative was my mother's only sibling, Alfred Brandt. Uncle Al was executive secretary to General Motors' Alfred P Sloan,

Jr. He was a bachelor who lived in a beautiful apartment on New York City's West End Avenue. He would come up to our house in Glen Rock on Christmas Eve with two suitcases filled with gifts. He didn't drive but I can remember that he left a 1927 Buick at our house-- also a 1930 Buick four-door convertible sedan with pigskin seats.

Uncle Al made it through the 1929 market crash, but lost his fortune when the banks went under in 1933. He contracted a kidney disease and died at a home in the Poconos at 44 years of age. He was a heavy hitter who knew and worked with the top people in industry and finance. I can remember going to a "Bon Voyage" party on the liner Europa before he sailed to Germany to represent General Motors. It must have been in the late twenties.

His funeral was held at our house in 1933. The "who's who" of business were there, including former Secretary of State Stettinius. My mother sent me away to camp on the Delaware River for two weeks while all this was going on.

My Uncle Al had a great influence on me. We had all of his personal things at our house after he passed away. With a small amount of money he had left to my mother, we got rid of the coal bin and the one big grate that heated our house and replaced them with oil heat and radiators. We had a sun porch built, and filled the book shelves with some fine literature. We received a few pieces of expensive furniture, glasses, and silverware.

In 1934 the depression really took hold and things got tough on my parents. As I had mentioned, my father at this time was a supervisor in the dye house. He came from the "old school." Most of his knowledge of the business came from years of hard work; experience was his main source for problem solving.

The workers in the silk mills were mostly Italian immigrants. They spoke very little English and, of course, had little or no education, so they were a prime target for labor unions. They became very difficult to control and my father fought them constantly. In fact, I remember one night he came home with a broken hand. He had smashed his fist on a wall in complete frustration.

The textile mills began closing in Paterson and moving south to get away from the unions. Further, craftsmen like my father were being replaced by chemists from textile colleges. The only thing my parents had was their house. My father got "black balled" by the unions and was out of work for seven years. He was a great hunter and fisherman—skills he used to keep earning some money for us by training hunting dogs and repairing shotguns and fishing equipment. I also helped with a paper route seven days a week in junior high and high school.

During the early 1940's, things slowly improved as my father got a job in a war plant and I worked while waiting to get into the Army Air Corps.

My mother was a very religious person and we lived about three plus miles from Mt. Carmel, the Catholic Church in Ridgewood. My brother told me she used to wheel me in a baby carriage to mass a couple mornings a week. She also made a perpetual Novena every Thursday to St Jude in Paterson and would take a bus down and back.

To understand my "old school" parents: the few times I ever missed school because of illness, my mother would come up to the bedroom, to put St Jude's oil on my forehead, and say, "Here Paul, this will help you get well, but don't tell your father." Then when my father would get home, he would come up to the bedroom and say, "What's the matter kid, don't you feel well? Here's a shot of whiskey. It will make you feel better but don't tell your mother."

Speaking of Mt Carmel, that is where I met the Van Tassel twins, Harry and Ed. We went to Sunday school together and made our Confirmations together. They were always well dressed and would come with Pop Dolan, their mother, and two little brothers every Sunday.

They attended Benjamin Franklin Junior High School in Ridgewood. The junior high students there got to use the high school gym, so those who wanted to play basketball had a big advantage in that sport over the rest of us. Our junior high coach arranged a soccer game with the ninth grade from Benjamin Franklin and they beat us by a wide margin.

We had heard about a player on that team who could kick a soccer ball like a pro and was a great athlete in all the major sports. We found out he lived up to his advance billing. It was Don Haldane, Bob's cousin. Don was six feet tall and weighed about 175 pounds with a powerful build. Even though we had no gym in Glen Rock, five of us put a team together and played them one Saturday morning at the Ridgewood YMCA. They beat us in a rout. Four of the players on their team were Don Haldane, Don McCullough, and the Van Tassel twins.

In eighth grade, I was the catcher on the baseball team. A seventh grader came along who was a terrific pitcher. His name was Harry Grundy. We became a virtually unbeatable team. In the summer when we didn't have a game we would take our lunch up to the Doremus Avenue ball field and practice together for five or six hours. He would throw fast balls, curves, change ups, and knuckle balls wherever I put the target. The baseball coach and athletic director at Ridgewood High came to see us play during my ninth grade year and we were a lock for the high school team. But more than that, my new-found Ben Franklin Junior High buddies wanted us on their American Legion team and that is how our life-long friendship began.

We were all pretty good students in high school and, of course, sports were a very important part of our lives. Back in those days, conditioning for student athletes didn't include weight lifting and other muscle-building aids that the high school athletes of today make a very important part of their training regimen. However, I must include an incident that took place early in my sophomore year at Ridgewood High. In the gym there was a heavy rope, maybe three inches wide, that hung from the ceiling which was probably 35 feet high. During physical education classes, we were asked to climb the rope hand-over-hand to the ceiling. Some of us couldn't do it. I was not able to get up more than a few feet. I was very embarrassed. Each night before I went home, I would look in the gym and, if no one was there, I would try to climb the rope – every time a little higher. Finally, I reached the ceiling. I heard some applause and I looked down. It was Duke

DeRochi, our athletic director and coach, who said to me, "Paul, I've watched you every night and I am very proud of you."

DeRochi was athletic director and baseball coach at Ridgewood High more than 20 years. I was very proud when he named me captain of the baseball team for my senior year. He also served as a Navy Lieutenant in WWII and participated in the landings at Iwo Jima.

At his retirement dinner in 1966, DeRochi was asked by the press, "In your years of coaching and as athletic director you must have had a couple thousand students go through your program; who were the top athletes on your teams?" Without hesitation he named for one sport Harry Grundy of Glen Rock, a right-handed pitcher who won more than 30 games during his three varsity years. His second pick for greatest all-round athlete was Don Haldane, a star in football, basketball, soccer, and baseball who was killed in action during WWII.

CHAPTER 3

The Cuba Incident

Harry and Ed VanTassel, Don McCullough, and I graduated from high school in June of 1941, a very confusing time of our lives. War was raging in Europe and the Pacific. Don and Bob Haldane and Walt Hays would be graduating a year later. We knew that, sooner or later, the United States might have to be involved so it was very difficult to plan on college or anything long range. The draft age was still 21 and our parents were not happy about signing off for us to get into the military. My father had been out of work for seven years so college didn't look like an option.

The rest of June, I was still playing semi-pro baseball. My pitcher buddy, Harry Grundy, still had another year of high school ahead of him so we would find time to practice at the Glen Rock AC Field. We had noticed an older man watching us for a couple days and he finally asked to talk with us. He was a Brooklyn Dodger scout and wanted us to go to Ebbets Field the next day for a tryout. He gave us a pass to get in the players' gate.

The following day we took a bus to the George Washington Bridge; walked across to the New York side and to the subway station. It cost ten cents for the subway to Brooklyn and ten cents for the ride back to the Bridge. That was all the money we had, along with a return ticket for the bus ride back home. We each had a bag to carry a mitt, baseball shoes, and a hat.

When we reached Ebbets Field, we went to a gate and the guard said. "This pass is only for one person." I told Harry he was the one they really wanted and I would wait for him in Prospect Park. Three hours went by and Harry finally arrived at the park. He was all smiles. He told me that he overheard Leo Durocher tell Larry Macphail that he was a $100,000 prospect and that he was invited back the next day for lunch and to pitch batting practice before the Phillie's game.

Incidentally, Harry was only 17 years old and many more major league teams would soon be interested in signing him.

* * * * * * * * * * * * *

Two weeks later my father told me he had found a job in Havana, Cuba through a newspaper ad and he wanted me to go with him. He would earn $65 dollars a week and he thought they had a university there that I could attend.

Dad in 1941

I got a job trucking boilers for a couple of weeks at Koven Boiler Works in Jersey City to earn a few bucks for the trip. In the middle of

July we headed for Havana in our 1939 Chevy. We arrived in Miami a few days later and boarded a ship for the overnight trip to Havana.

The next morning we docked in Havana. A man named Menendez found us and told us that he owned the dye house in Marianao, Cuba, where my father would be working and that we could find a room at the Nacionale Hotel in Havana. We checked in and went to the room; it was a disaster. There wasn't a chance that we could stay there. We found a newspaper published in English and noticed a room for rent in the Vedado section of town. We called and the woman told us the rent would be 35 pesos a month, so we said we would take it. We checked out of the hotel and I said, "Pop, how much money do we have left?" He said "fifteen dollars"; and that is when I decided I was on my own. High school days were over and it was time to get serious about moving on and making plans for the future.

It was dark when we arrived at the house. We took the steamer trunk out of the car. The good news was the house didn't look that bad. We started up the stairs and the woman, who really didn't speak English, told us to stop: we had to pay in advance. My father, who could barely speak Italian let alone Spanish, asked for a phone book and looked up Menendez. There were about 500 of them. Luckily we found him and he told the woman he would give us the money the next day so that we could pay her the first month's rent.

The room was only big enough for a double bed but it was clean. There was only one bathroom for the three bedrooms but it too was clean. I finally figured out that the other people were refugees from Europe who were escaping the Nazis. Now I was beginning to get the picture what the outside world was all about. I had to forget about the University of Havana. We had to figure out how we could save enough out of the $65 a week, after $35 a month rent and two meals a day in a cheap restaurant, for the boat back to Miami and the ride back to New Jersey where I could get a job, put food on the table, and go to night school. I turned 18 on July 27, 1941, in Cuba but it felt more like 35.

We went to the dye shop the next day in Marianao and it was a tiny little "dump." When Pop saw one of his workers, (there were sixteen in all) finish a cigarette, step on the butt, and leap into the air in pain because he had no sole in his shoe, he was easy to convince that my plan to leave was the only option.

Pop loved to play the horses so we budgeted a few dollars to bet at Oriental Park on weekends. A few weeks into August he said to me, "I want to bet two dollars on this eighty-to-one shot to win." I agreed and as luck would have it, the horse won! Now we had enough money to buy the tickets and get home.

We were a little nervous that we might run into trouble because my father had had to sign papers that made him a resident of Cuba. There was a huge crowd getting on the ship. Our old car had been put in the hold of the ship. There was barely enough room for us on the deck because it was so crowded with refugees who were trying to get away from Germany and Italy by way of Cuba. And we were still concerned about getting through customs in Miami.

We arrived in the morning, cleared through customs without any problems, and began our return trip to New Jersey. We never stopped except for gasoline, food, and water.

* * * * * * * * * * * * *

When we arrived home, I immediately applied for work at Wright Aeronautical and got a job at the Cylinder Head Foundry in Fairlawn, New Jersey—on the graveyard shift, midnight to eight AM. Then I found out that the VanTassel twins had jobs on the same shift at Botany Worsted Mills and had purchased an old Dodge sedan. The three of us entered night school at Bergen Jr. College. Classes began at seven PM and ended at ten thirty. This gave me time to get home, grab a ten minute nap and head for work. Incidentally, working in the foundry was very tough. I inspected cylinder heads, helped pour hot molten metal into the molds, and knocked the molds off the finished heads. I did this for ten months.

* * * * * * * * * * * * *

My friend Harry Grundy, who was still in high school, called me a few days after I arrived home from Cuba and told me he had forced his dad to let him sign with the Dodgers. He wanted to show me his car. It was a 1934 Chevy convertible with no top. I said "Harry, how much did you pay for it?" Harry said "Seventy five dollars that's what the Dodgers paid me to sign." Talk about a bad decision!

The next year he would win another dozen high school games, make All State, and five major league teams would try to sign him-- but the Dodgers owned him. He was drafted after he graduated from high school and after three years of military service, pitched in the Dodger farm system, but never got any higher than Triple A ball. A tough lesson in life!

* * * * * * * * * * * * *

I really wanted to tell this story about the trip to Cuba because it was a very important lesson for me. It convinced me that I needed to get a college degree. I had to work while getting it to pay the bills. Every person doesn't get the same deal in life. Some have it given to them and some have to earn it. Look out for the guy who has to earn it. He just might have the character to pull it off and be a huge success.

CHAPTER 4

1941 – A Year
That Changed My Life

I had already graduated from high school, had spent several months in Cuba, had gone to work in Wright Aeronautical, and had begun night school at Bergen Jr. College. All this time the world was in turmoil because of the military ambition of Axis powers Germany, Japan, and Italy.

The United States found itself at the center of this out-of-control situation. Our allies were being beaten or threatened by power-grabbing criminals, and our nation was divided between "America First" people and those who wanted us to go to the aid of our allies.

On December 7, 1941, the decision was made for our country. It was a cold, dreary day in North Jersey. After mass, my brother Henry said, "Let's go up to Caldwell Airport and I'll teach you how to fly an airplane." I agreed to go with him because he had recently received his pilot's license and was flying Piper Cubs. The Piper was a small two- seat plane and Hank had less than 100 hours flying time. He had always loved airplanes and his ambition was to be an airline pilot.

* * * * * * * * * * * *

In 1936 and 1937, he had taken me to the Cleveland Air Races so that we could watch the Thompson Trophy races where Jimmy Doolittle flew the famous Gee Bee plane against the top pilots of his time. He won those races around closed-course pylons at speeds of more than 200 miles per hour.

In the early thirties Hank and his friends, who loved airplanes, put up a cable between two trees—about 30 feet in the air and 50 yards long. They hung a box on the cable with two clothes-line pulleys to hold it up. Since I was the lightest, I was selected for the first ride after the cable had been greased. They dropped a rope down through the box and had pulled me about half way when the pulleys split and I was hanging by two screws. So much for my first solo flight! They had to go get a ladder to bring me down. During those early years Hank passed his passion for flying on to me, and Jimmie Doolittle was my idol.

* * * * * * * * * * * * *

Now, eight years later, Hank had his pilot's license and was ready to give me a lesson. After an hour in the air we landed. On the ride home we turned on the car radio and found that the Japanese had attacked Pearl Harbor.

Our lives would never be the same. Ninety days later Hank was an Ensign in the Naval Air Corps teaching Navy cadets how to fly. He was 24 years old. I was 18 and I wanted to get into the Army Air Corps as a pilot. There were two things standing in my way. The first was that you had to have two years of college; the second was that "Pop" wouldn't sign off for me to enlist.

One of my closest friends, Bob Haldane, had entered the military program at VPI in the summer of 1942. He said, "Why don't you come down here? You can room with me and, with your night school credits, get the two years of college that you need to get into the Air Corps." My family had no money for tuition and expenses, so I got my father to sign off on a small loan using as collateral my $6500 that I would get when I was 21 (a gift from Uncle Al). In September of 1942, I headed for VPI with Bob Haldane.

My major was Mechanical Engineering, and after about three weeks I discovered that I hated it. Mechanical drawing and chemistry were not my style, and close-order drill and marching in dress parades were not my "cup of tea" either.

One day in October, we received notice that the Army Air Corps was coming to the campus and would be giving an IQ test for pilot training. You could bypass the two-year requirement if your IQ was high enough. The military also announced that in the near future they would be drafting 18 year olds.

I arranged to go back to New Jersey for Thanksgiving because I had received a letter from the Army Air Corps that I had passed the IQ test, and I felt that I now could convince "Pop" to sign off. He still objected, but when I told him I was leaving Sunday for Roanoke, Virginia, to be sworn into the Army Air Corps on Monday at 9:00AM; showed him the papers, and explained that the draft age would be lowered to eighteen, he gave in.

Monday morning I was on my way to those coveted Silver Wings. All I had to do was wait for my orders and then earn them. I finished the semester, and during the second semester my orders finally came. Bob enlisted a month later.

Pillars of Character

Iinterrupt my largely personal history to give you more details about the men who had assembled in the Dolans' living room to discuss their futures so long ago.

I have become involved with the Mighty Eighth Air Force Museum in a youth educational program called "Character Counts!" It seeks to create awareness and active pursuit of six universally accepted traits critical to good character: Trustworthiness, Respect, Responsibility, Fairness, Caring, and Citizenship.

The six pillars of "Character Counts", as developed by the Josepheson Institute of Ethics, are further explained below:

TRUSTWORTHINESS: Integrity often requires courage – a firmness of spirit that enables us to try new things, pursue new goals, persevere, overcome fears.

RESPECT: Value and honor all people for themselves and not what they can do for you.

RESPONSIBILITY: What you do and don't do matters. "If you can't change your situation, change your attitude."

FAIRNESS: Fairness involves actions, processes, and consequences that are morally right, honorable, and equitable.

CARING: Show love, regard, and concern for the well being of others.

CITIZENSHIP: It's not just about country, but about your home, school and community as well.

I believe that the lives of these men illustrate the six pillars of Character Counts perfectly. The fact of the matter is, they each could have fit all six. To emphasize the importance of each pillar, I chose to select one for each of the character points. The following six chapters let you see the consistent presence of these traits throughout their lives.

"There is a mysterious cycle in human events.

To some generations much is given.
Of other generations much is expected.

This generation of Americans
has a Rendezvous with Destiny."

Franklin D. Roosevelt

CHAPTER 5

Trustworthiness
WALT HAYS – "ED" OR "RED"

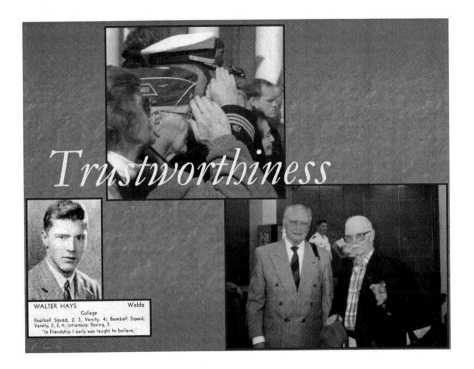

WALTER HAYS   Waldo
College
Football Squad, 2, 3, Varsity, 4; Baseball Squad,
Varsity, 2, 3, 4; Intramural Boxing, 3.
"In friendship I early was taught to believe."

Again, each of my six friends could have fit each of the pillars of character. However, I selected the one that I felt was the most applicable and for Walt: Trustworthiness.

In June of 1945 I received a 30-day leave. The war in Europe had just ended and I was headed for B29 training in anticipation of being sent to bomb the Japanese homeland. We had flown our B24 from England, via Iceland, Labrador, Maine to Bradley Field Conn. We cleared through Ft. Dix; then I headed home to Glen Rock, where my family was still living. I arrived home Sunday night and after some idle "chit chat" with my mom and pop, I went to bed to catch up on some sleep.

Early Monday morning, I was awakened by mom shouting "Paul – Wally's here!" I ran down stairs and there was Walt Hays in his uniform. He had just arrived home the night before and was on a 60-day leave. I quickly cleaned up and dressed. We never discussed where we had been or what we had done – just got in the car, parked at the New York bus stop and headed for Manhattan.

Walt and I got off at the Broadway and Forty Second St. stop and went into the Cross Roads Tavern. We still didn't do much talking – mostly reminiscing about old times—then walked to the Hotel New Yorker at Thirty Third St and Eighth Ave. We decided to have a drink at each bar along the way but only on one side of the street.

We sat for a while at the hotel; then decided that we would call Louise Schweinler, our pal Don Haldane's fiancée whom we hadn't seen since Don was killed in his F6F. She said, "I'll be right there." We hadn't seen her for years and she invited us up to her mom's apartment on Riverside Drive. We said "Let's go!"

* * * * * * * * * * * * *

Louise, her mom, and two sisters, Marie and Helen, had lived there ever since our high school days. Mrs. Schweinler was a terrific person and their large home in Ridgewood, NJ was a place where my friends and I were always welcome during our high school days. Their big apartment in New York City was no different. I had dated Marie Schweinler when I was a senior in high school and just before we enlisted. I was dating her while Don Haldane was dating Louise.

I'll never forget what Mrs. Schweinler told me when I was visiting there one day while on leave. We were talking about what I might do, if and when I returned from the war, and she said, "It doesn't matter what you do, even if it's shining shoes; just work as hard as you can. Put your heart and soul into it and you will be successful."

* * * * * * * * * * * * *

Walt, Louise and I at a subway "Fotomat"

The three of us hopped on the subway and went to the apartment on Riverside Drive, where we sat with the four ladies, talked and answered questions all night and into the morning about our war-time experiences. Walt told us about that fateful day February 24, 1944, when his plane, a B17 "Just Elmer's Tune," was returning from a raid on Poznan. They were jumped on by a squadron of Me109s.

WALT HAYS

Walt was in the tail turret. One of the Me109's making a pass at them had badly damaged the B17. It flew by the tail and Walt, the sharp shooter that he was, nailed the German fighter. They were at 13,000 feet when the co-pilot rang the "abandon ship" alarm; his pilot had been severely wounded.

Walt bailed out and landed in a tree. The co-pilot decided to crash-land the B17 because the pilot was not able to jump with a parachute. A 15-year-old Dane cut Walt down from the tree and wheeled him on his bike to the nearest hospital so they could treat his injuries.

While he was being cared for, the German pilot, Sinnecker, was brought into the hospital for his injuries. Denmark was occupied by the Germans and the hospital was under their control, so the Danes introduced the two of them while they were both hospitalized.

Two of the crew of "Just Elmer's Tune" were killed—the navigator and the flight engineer. The rest of the crew were in bad shape and, after some treatment, they became POW's. The pilot had been hit with flak and, under primitive conditions, had many pieces of metal removed from his body. Some had gone through a lung and seven pieces couldn't be removed. The operation was done without anesthesia. The only pain killer available was a glass of cognac.

Walt was interrogated by the Luftwaffe; and, a couple days later, was loaded into a boxcar crowded with POWs headed for an unknown destination. It was freezing cold. The trip lasted six days. Most of the prisoners were ill and a number died from the flu and other diseases while still suffering from wounds they had received from being shot down or crash landing.

Walt was a prisoner for 18 months. He told of many things that happened relating to those terrible conditions—like slicing the bread very thin to search for broken glass before they ate it; slop for food; and contending with rats and other vermin.

He was among those who were transferred to Stalag One in Barth, Germany. He finally was put in a forced march, handcuffed to a fellow POW for two weeks. They were prodded along by German bayonets. There were 8,000 of them whom the Germans wanted to offer to the Russians as hostages. Walt said that his weight had gone down to 85 pounds. He also said to us, "Freedom is like the air we breathe; ingrained in each moment, it is soon forgotten. But taken away for an instant, its significance becomes immediately clear."

* * * * * * * * * * * * *

After we had told enough stories for our gracious hostesses, we took a nap and when we woke up Mrs. Schweinler had prepared a fine breakfast for us. The table was decorated with pretty flowers in honor of our return to civilization.

We told the girls that we were going down to Riverside Drive, would hitch-hike a ride to the George Washington Bridge bus stop, and return to New Jersey. In those days hitching a ride while in uniform was easy, and the girls hung a white sheet out of the window to let us know when we were on the right spot to get a ride. When we got home, our families never asked us where we had been for a day and a half. I guess they figured it would take some time to get our recent pasts out of our system.

We had a lot of catching up to do for 30 days. The war was still raging in the Pacific, and for some of us, B29 training was on the horizon. Those who had been prisoners of war had a 60-day leave and were assigned more rehab at military bases. It was a unique time for us who were returning from Europe. Every day more of our friends were returning and waiting to be redeployed or reassigned.

Walt and I spent quite a lot of time at a public golf course called Saddle River, not far from where we lived. Unknown to me, Bobby Woods was a bombardier in my Bomb Group. His father owned the course and we had a place to have some fun and watch the bombers coming back from Europe. They passed over Bergen County from Bradley Field, Conn. on their way to the junk yard in Pima, Arizona. We had a chance to figure out from the tail markings what friends of ours might soon be joining us for the rest of our leave.

* * * * * * * * * * * * *

Walt continued earning the position as the "Trustworthiness" pillar of Character Counts after he was discharged from the service. He and his wife Joan were married in 1947. They have three children, five grand children, and two great grand children. Walt had his own printing business and was very active in the Ex-Prisoners of War Organization where he was Commander and National Service Officer. He helped his fellow ex-prisoners of war get their benefits from the Veteran's Administration. He made many speeches at McGuire Air Base Non-Commissioned Officers Academy, schools, veteran's groups, and service organizations. He became an excellent speaker.

On May 12, 1995, The Danish American Society invited Walt Hays and his wife to a dinner dance at the New York Yacht Club where he was to be the guest speaker. The other honored guest speaker was the famous Danish entertainer Victor Borge. The dinner dance was in honor of American Veterans of World War II. His Royal Highness Prince Joachim, the great grandson of King Christian X of Denmark, was in attendance. King Christian X was on the coin that the Dane who cut Walt down from the tree showed him to prove that he had landed in Denmark. In his speech that evening, Walt thanked all the Danish patriots that had helped him and his crew survive their ordeal.

Walt cuts ribbon at POW museum opening

Walt and Joan made a couple more trips to Denmark, and on the June, 1998 trip, took along their daughter Susan, their grandchild Allison, and great grandchild Vanessa. This was a very special trip because after Denmark, they were going to Berlin for a meeting with the German pilot, Sinnecker, who had shot Walt down.

The Sinneckers and their granddaughter met the Hays family and Fritz Ulrich at the airport. The ladies were given red roses and then took an automobile tour of Berlin. Then to Sinnecker's apartment in the Siemens section of Berlin. The German pilot had made his career with Siemens Electronics after WWII. They had a nice visit and spent most of the time discussing current events. They both knew what happened that day in 1944 and immediately following. Ironically, the German became an allied POW toward the end of WWII in Europe and was liberated about the same time as Walt.

What an amazing meeting for these two men and their families! Fifty-four years before, they were mortal enemies, trying to kill each other over the skies of Denmark, and here they are introducing themselves to their loved ones. Walt called me before he left and said, "Paul – I'm trying to think of what I should say to him." And I said, "Walt you will think of something appropriate – you gave him a pretty good answer over Denmark."

* * * * * * * * * * * * *

For more than 50 years, Walt and his family, General Haldane and his family, and I and my family exchanged Holiday cards and corresponded with each other. Walt stayed involved with the Ex-POW program and of course Lt. General Haldane served in the Military for 40 years.

I had become very involved with the Mighty Eighth Air Force Museum in Savannah and was Commander of the Eighth Air Force Historical Society. We were having a dinner meeting at the Mighty Eighth Air Force Museum for the Twenty Fifth Reunion of the Historical Society, so I decided it would be great to have my two life-long buddies as the guest speakers. They both accepted and of course their wives accompanied them.

My speakers were terrific. Among the 300 attendees, we had eight retired generals. We had a great time, played a couple rounds of golf, and traded a myriad of stories. We had excellent media coverage and I was very proud of my 70-year-old-plus pals. Here we are, three life-long friends enjoying a game of golf in Savannah GA.

*Paul, Bob and Walt**

Walt was a very trustworthy person. He kept his promises and above all was loyal to his family, his friends, and his country. He was a great soldier who now lies in rest at the National Cemetery in Arlington, VA.

---

* For more details of Walt Hays' wartime experience see *A Rendezvous with Destiny* by Fritz Ulrich. Lt. General Bob Haldane in the Foreword of the book says *"This book tells the stories of some involved in the war, members of the United States Eighth Army Air Force, the Luftwaffe, and brave Danes who risked (and sometimes lost) their lives assisting downed Allied airmen to escape or at least survive. This is a work of love, but it is also invaluable as a record for posterity, facts that present and future generations should know and remember. They should not be unaware of the sacrifices of past generations."*

CHAPTER 6

Respect
'POP' DOLAN

Pop Dolan with his two stepsons

Ifirst met his two oldest sons, Harry and Ed Van Tassel, when I attended Mt Carmel Church in Ridgewood, New Jersey. Mass was at nine o'clock, and Mr. and Mrs. Dolan would walk into the church followed by their four boys, Ed, Harry, Bill, and Walt. Mr. Dolan was always well-dressed, carrying a "Homburg" hat and his mass missal, and wearing a dark suit, white shirt and tie. He usually had a white handkerchief neatly folded in his lapel pocket.

* * * * * * * * * * * * *

During a visit to the Mighty Eighth Museum here in Savannah, July 28, 2005, his son Bill gave us an oral history about his dad and this is some of what he said.

"My father was of Irish descent and he loved Ireland. But above all he was an American and was very proud to be an American. There were Dolans in the Revolutionary War, and I think that a sense of duty ran in my father's blood. He felt things but he didn't express them outwardly—he did it by action.

During the thirties he was CEO of an importing firm based in New York City. They imported very fine foods from European countries and distributed them around the United States. It was a very successful business. However, when Hitler crossed the Polish border in 1939, it was obvious that there would be no more exports from Europe.

As the war began to rage he quietly contacted General Spaatz with whom he had served in the Lafayette Escadrille in WWI. Spaatz told him to stay home- it was a young man's war. My dad inwardly believed that he could make a contribution to the war effort and that he had a lot to offer. He was a persistent man. He did not give up. In the spring of 1942 a telegram arrived from the War Department with a commission as Captain. He never told us that he had been trying to enlist. His orders were to report to a new bomb group that was just forming – the 384th. Its commander was Bud Peasley, and Pop Dolan was his first recruit. He later served four more commanders in this group."

Pop Dolan was named Intelligence Officer of the 384th Bomb Group, and he was the only person who served in the group from the beginning to the end of the war in Europe. Intelligence officers led the briefing sessions for the airmen preparing to fly the day's mission. They described the target and related the type of enemy airplanes that group would encounter, along with the time, place, and altitude at all points of the operation. They discussed the headings from the initial point and along the bomb run to the target, as well as what to do if shot down in enemy territory. These and other details were covered by intelligence on every mission before take-off.

Pop Dolan also took over the chaplain's duties as the 384th did not as yet have a chaplain assigned to them. In addition to publishing the base newspaper "Plane Talk," he flew nine early missions as an intelligence officer so that he would know first-hand what the flyers faced.

* * * * * * * * * * * * *

In his later years, Pop Dolan recalled that in World War I there was an element of mutual respect among pilots of both sides. Regarding the armistice signed on November 11, 1918 that ended the Great War, Dolan commented, "That marked the end of an era. The French, British, and Americans all loved each other. Even the Germans were conceded a certain tragic grandeur by our American pilots. There was a good bit of camaraderie then."

"When I was intelligence officer in World War II, I always told the pilots, 'If you get shot down and can't evade capture, try to get to Luftwaffe airfields. There is a certain amount of understanding on their part. Above all, avoid the Hitler youth; the kids are the worst.'" He noted that time had changed the world of aviation he knew. "Even the people have changed," Dolan said. "Young people today are entirely different."

* * * * * * * * * * * * *

Bill, your father had three great attributes: what he did for his country, his family, and his faith.

I believe the values we are trying to teach here at the Museum are the values your father taught me, you, your brothers, our friends, and those young airmen from the 384th Bomb Group. He gave us those values and we didn't know we were getting them. But we got them and weren't afraid to do the job that we set out to do. We hope that here at the Museum we can teach those values to the young people who come through; and if only a few catch on, we have done our job. I feel very strongly that today we need more and more of those values to be passed on to the young people.

Respect goes both ways. If you show respect for other people, those people will respect you in return. On the other hand, if you show disrespect for other people, there is no chance that they will respect you. Pop Dolan was not only a fine military man and leader but he taught respect in all phases of his life. His stepsons respected him, his biological sons respected him, my friends and I respected him, and the 384th Bomb Group respected him.

There is not one person whom I have met coming through the Mighty Eighth from the 384th Bomb Group that I haven't asked, "Did you know 'Pop' Dolan?" And they all answer, "Did I know 'Pop' Dolan? Everyone in the 384th knew 'Pop' Dolan. Not only because he was recognized as one of the top intelligence officers in the Mighty Eighth, but because he was the heart and soul of that Bomb Group."

This picture of Colonel Dolan appeared in a book he had published so the 384th Bomb Group would never be forgotten. It is entitled *"as briefed"*, and it gives a detailed account of the 384th from the beginning of its formation through the end of the air war in Europe. Its caption is, "But it was 'Pop' Dolan, only staff officer to serve the Group through the entire period, who was the embodiment of the spirit of the 384th Bomb Group." He was truly admired by his fellow airmen at Grafton Underwood.

* * * * * * * * * * * * *

Our Museum received a great deal of memorabilia from his "War Room" in Cooperstown NY that "Pop's" youngest son maintained for him. The documents we have put together tell a story of what he accomplished while serving in two world wars. In addition, he saw to it that the town of Grafton Underwood would never forget those brave Americans who served there. Colonel Dolan did a great deal after WWII as well to keep the group's achievements alive and never to let those who fought and died for our freedom be forgotten.

The next picture is a water color of different scenes of English churches, villages, monuments, and quonset huts that were near the 384th's base in Northhamtonshire during WWII. The uniform patches of the 544th, 545th, 546th and 547th Bomb Squadrons are in the corners of the painting. The Kettering Parish Church, The Royal Hotel Pub, and the Monument to the 384th are featured also.

This painting is a gift to the 384th Bombardment Group from the
congregation of Kettering Parish Church. It was painted by Yvonne

Worthington and was presented to visiting Americans who, during WWII, served with the USAF at Grafton Underwood. The presentation took place during a service of commemoration and thanksgiving for the American contributions in England, and in the presence of her Royal Highness, Princess Alice, Duchess of Gloucester. "Pop" Dolan attended the ceremony and had copies of the painting made for each of his children. His daughter-in-law, Laurie Van Tassel, gave hers to the Mighty Eighth Museum.

* * * * * * * * * * * *

This is a picture of then-Captain Dolan with Pilot Herb Schaaf and nine members of his B17 crew. Dolan was an observer on this flight because he was the Group's Chief Intelligence Officer. He is sitting second from the left in parachute harness and cold weather boots.

Herb Schaaf is standing on the far right. Herb Schaaf finished up a colonel. I got to know him at the Mighty Eighth Air Force Historical

Society. Herb was the first Wing Commander of the Savannah Wing. I was the Wing Commander a couple years later. We became friends and he told me some great stories about "Pop" Dolan. One of them: When Herb was promoted to Captain from First Lieutenant he was on a rest leave in Scotland. "Pop" flew up to tell him that he had been promoted. He gave Herb his own captain's bars and a quart of Scotch to celebrate.

"Pop" Dolan flew nine missions during those early tough days with hardly any fighter escorts to find out what his men were going through. It's very difficult to imagine what would have happened if he'd had to bail out and become a POW at 55 years of age.

* * * * * * * * * * * * *

Colonel Dolan gave a silver chalice to Kettering's St. Edward's Roman Catholic Church where he worshipped while stationed there. The chalice is set with his deceased wife's diamond engagement ring.

The Silver Chalice presented by William Dolan to St. Edwards Roman Catholic Church, Kettering, England. Dedicated in honor of the 384th Bomb Group.

We have more than 120 pieces of memorabilia in our archives at the Mighty Eighth Air Force Museum. This last picture is of "Pop" Dolan with his Mae West life preserver after taking a ride in an F86 jet fighter. He was about 70 years old at the time. He is with his son Walt who served in the Air Force.

The Colonel not only earned respect – he commanded respect.

CHAPTER 7

Responsibility
LT. GENERAL
ROBERT HALDANE

Responsibility

General Robert Haldane's service and life exemplified the standards he held so dear:

WEST POINT:

Duty, Honor, Country

First Infantry Division, the Big Red One

No mission too difficult

No sacrifices too great

Duty first.

ROBERT HALDANE   Bob
Virginia Military Institute
Baseball Assistant Manager, 3. Manager, 4; Student
Council, 3; Home Room President, 3.
"O, what man within him hide,
Though angel on the outward side!"

Bob Haldane and I were life-long friends. We got to know each other very well in junior high school and high school. We both had grown up in Glen Rock, NJ, and in those days middle school or junior high was 7th, 8th and 9th grades; high school was 10th, 11th, and 12th grades. Glen Rock had no high school at that time so it was a big move when we began high school at Ridgewood.

That was a large challenge for the kids from the small towns that surrounded Ridgewood. The competition was intense. Ridgewood was one of the highest rated high schools in the state. More than 90 percent of those who attended went on to college and this is still the case.

But the years that we attended there were special because the world was in turmoil and war was raging all around us. Though it all, we did the things that most young people always did while growing up. We studied hard to keep our grade point average up so we could be accepted at a college or university. We played sports, had fun, and went out on dates. I didn't have an allowance and knew better than to ask my parents for money because they didn't have it, so I earned it with my seven-day-a- week paper route. No one worried about whether your family was well off or not—a friend was a friend.

We played ice hockey in the winter, sometimes all day long. In the summer we played baseball and in the fall football. Bob wasn't the greatest athlete but he played with us and tried the hardest of anyone to play well. When we were in high school he became manager of the baseball team and was on the student council. He was a very bright student and got excellent marks.

Another thing he was very good at was attracting pretty girls. When he was old enough to drive, his parents got him a nice red convertible that we double-dated in. I can remember several times when his dad would say, "Hey Bob, here's five dollars and another for your pal Paul. Be careful and have a good time." However, you will soon find out that Bob Haldane became the toughest of the tough during his long military career, a great soldier and leader of men.

In Bob's memoirs to his youngest daughter he said, "Halfway through my senior year in high school WWII began—an event that influenced many lives. I decided to go to military college and went to VPI in June of 1942."

I joined him there in September, and we were roommates for about one and a half semesters until I got my orders from the Air Force. Bob finished his freshmen year at VPI and immediately volunteered for the draft. Despite his protests that he wanted to be in the infantry, he was assigned to the Air Corps, and after training was sent to England. He was assigned to a liaison squadron equipped with Piper Cubs. These were eventually used as spotter planes for air and artillery strikes. His job was to conduct daily tests of the radio in each plane, not challenging or satisfying work.

In late November, 1943, he was advised that he was going back to the USA to enter West Point. He returned to the United States to begin a military career that would span 40 years. Bob was in the class of 1947 and WWII ended in September of 1945. We maintained our friendship, and while I was at Lafayette we had Army on our baseball schedule. When we arrived for the game in the spring of 1946, Cadet Haldane was our escort for the day and he was there again in 1947, his senior year.

BOB HALDANE

Bob graduated from West Point and had a brilliant career in the military. So that we understand how important he was to the men that were in combat with him and served under him during his many years of service, I use some documents that were written about his leadership. It is obvious that Lt. General Haldane was a soldier's soldier.

In March of 2007, Nancy and I were guests of the Haldanes at their home in Alexandria, Virginia. We were there to attend Walt Hay's funeral at Arlington National Cemetery. After the funeral the four of us—Bob, Elise, Nancy and I—visited the Aero Space Museum near Dulles Airport. While walking around the facility Bob said to me, "Hey Grass, see that helicopter up there? I won 17 Air Medals, two Distinguished Flying Crosses, and two Silver Stars out of one of those." Of course he never told me all the other medals he had been awarded and that the two Silver Stars were for bravery. Little did we know that in just a year we would be attending Bob's funeral at Arlington Cemetery with all the "Pomp and Circumstance" that a Lt. General receives.

In April of 2012, Elise sent me a note that included the memoir Bob had written to his youngest daughter Bobbi. She also said that her family had not known what Bob had done during his two tours in Vietnam until after he died. After his funeral, they made a notebook about him for each of his children and grandchildren. She sent me a copy and it certifies the kind of person that General Haldane was—a quiet humble man who was a great soldier and leader of men. Those who served under him really saw first-hand what a powerful force he was.

Here are two of Bob's favorite quotations that he carried with him during his many assignments all over the world:

"It is not the critic who counts, not the man who points out how the strong man stumbled, or where the doer of deeds could have done them better. The credit belongs to the man who is actually in the arena, whose face is marred by dust and sweat and blood; who strives valiantly, who errs and comes short again and again; who knows the great enthusiasms, the great devotions, and spends himself in a worthy cause; who, at the best, knows in the end the triumph of high achievement; and who, at the worst, if he fails, at

least fails while daring greatly, so that his place shall never be with those cold and timid souls who know neither victory nor defeat"

Credited to Theodore Roosevelt

A ROMAN GENERAL'S OPINON OF MILITARY CRITICS 2137 Years Ago

LUCIOUS AEMILIUS PAULUS, A Roman Consul, who had been selected to conduct the war with the Macedonians, B. C. 168, went out from the Senate-house into the assembly of the people and addressed them as follows:

"In every circle, and truly, at every table, there are people who lead armies into Macedonia; who know where the camp ought to be placed; what posts ought to be occupied by troops; when and through what pass that territory should be entered: where magazines should be formed; how provisions should be conveyed by land and sea; and when it is proper to engage the enemy, when to lie quiet. And not only determine what is to be done, but if anything is done in any other manner than what they pointed out, they arraign the consul, as if they were on trial before them.

"These are great impediments to those who have the management of affairs; for everyone cannot encounter injurious reports with the same constancy and firmness of mind as Fabius did, who chose to let his own ability be questioned through the folly of the people, rather than to mismanage the public business with a high reputation.

"I am not one of those who think that commanders ought at no time to receive advice; on the contrary, I should deem that man more proud than wise who regulated every proceeding by the standard of his own single judgment.

"What then is my opinion? That commanders should be counseled chiefly by persons of known talent; by those who have made the art of war their particular study, and whose

knowledge is derived from experience; from those who are present at the scene of action, who see the country, who see the enemy; who see the advantages that occasions offer, and who, like people embarked in the same ship, are sharers of the danger.

"If, therefore, anyone thinks himself qualified to give advice respecting the war which I am to conduct, which may prove advantageous to the public, let him not refuse his assistance to the state, but let him come with me to Macedonia. He shall be furnished with a ship, a horse, a tent; even his traveling charges will be defrayed. But if he thinks this too much trouble, and prefers the repose of a city life to the toils of war, let him not, on land, assume the office of a pilot. The city, in itself furnishes abundance of topics for conversation; let it confine its passion for talking within its own precincts, and rest assured that we shall pay no attention to my councils but what shall be framed within our camp."

Livy, *History of Rome*, Vo. 7, Book XLIV, Chapter 22, Translation by George Baker, AM

Here is what Larry Peterson, LTC, USA Retired, said about General Haldane in a letter to Elise.

"My last flight in Vietnam was with General Haldane while he was serving as Brigade Commander. He was giving me a bad time about being a helicopter pilot that day but he said he would take it easy and not fly a lot. As I remember we had lunch at his CP and he gave me some good military career advice. Toward the end of the day he suggested that we make one quick flight over his troops in the field and then he would release the aircraft. No sooner had we gotten into the air but one of his units reported heavy contact. Without hesitation he directed us to fly him to the contact point. When we arrived, the ground commander had been badly wounded and needed evacuation. When on the ground to evacuate the

commander, General Haldane left the helicopter with my two door machine guns and went to command the fight on the ground. As I remember he stayed on the ground with the unit in contact until the fight was over some six hours later. This was typical of General Haldane."

Colonel Peterson said the following after he retired from the Pentagon in 1989:

"I have thought of General Haldane often and I wished I had communicated with him about how much he had been a part of my life. I am now teaching eighth graders U.S. History in Lincoln, Nebraska. I share with my students, when I can fit it into the stories, about the type of men like General Haldane and what they have given for their country.

"General Haldane's gentle kindness, soft gentle smile, and unequaled wisdom will be with me always. I am a better person having had the opportunity of serving with your husband."

Patricia Sullivan, Washington Post staff writer, wrote this in Bob's Obituary:

"Colonel Haldane's unit discovered the Cu Chi Tunnels. He ordered red smoke grenades dropped into the entrance and within minutes, reports came in from every direction of red smoke appearing from holes in the ground, according to Infantry in Vietnam(1967) edited by Albert N. Garland. The smoke didn't rout the enemy, so Colonel Haldane ordered his troops to pump in CS, a non-lethal control gas. The Viet Cong stayed put. Finally, Sgt. Green went in with a demolitions specialist, placed explosive charges, and hustled out of the tunnel before the earth exploded. It turned out there were 125 miles of tunnels, filled with supplies and equipment, that were later the scene of hand-to-hand combat as American "tunnel rats" fought the Viet Cong in the dark and vermin-infested earth.

Even as the tunnels were being discovered, fierce fighting raged in the area. General Haldane was awarded the Silver Star for his actions January 16, 1966, when he rushed an enemy position while under fire to give first aid to wounded troops. The Viet Cong blocked his efforts to evacuate the wounded. His Silver Star citation said that, armed only with a .45 caliber pistol, Lieutenant Colonel Haldane fearlessly charged the principal Viet Cong strong point, firing his weapon as he ran forward. His dauntless courage inspired his men to continue the assault, and ensured the successful evacuation of the casualties, as well as the seizure of the objective.

General Haldane served a second tour in Vietnam in 1968 as commander of the 3rd Brigade of the first Infantry Division."

If you "Google" General Haldane's name you will see "A Salute to LTG Robert Haldane" by CW3(Ret) Ricardo M. Cantu. He has written about the General and tells what he thought of him and how great a leader he was. Here are a few excerpts from that article.

"I served a number of outstanding commanders during my 22 years in the Army. In terms of military tactical competence and earning respect, I rate General Haldane at the very top of my list. I served under his command in Vietnam from April, 1969, until his departure in August 1969. I was his brigade food adviser.

During the dinner meal he wanted to know all about me. I told him my story – the short version being that I entered the Army as a young Mexican-American boy with a fourth grade education. Through dedication, hard work, and great mentors, I had succeeded in the Army to that point being appointed a Chief Warrant Officer. From that time on, we became very close. Almost on a daily basis he would alert his driver to go get me, and I would fly with him, or he would pull over in front of my office and holler at me, 'Chief, get out here, and let's go!'

"I became a regular passenger on his command chopper, and as a result, I am a first-hand witness to his tactical genius and personal courage. During a very serious battle, Colonel Haldane was aware that an engineer platoon had been ambushed and several soldiers were wounded and needed evacuation. Without a medivac in the area, he directed his pilot to the location. When the pilot landed the aircraft the only individuals left behind were the pilot and the door gunners. The rest of us, including Colonel Haldane, left the chopper and took cover to give maximum room to evacuate the wounded soldiers. If he had any fear, it never showed. He led from the front and was a soldier's soldier."

A few weeks ago while taking my early morning exercises at our fitness center, one of my fellow fitness friends, Tom Donahue, whom I knew was a West Point graduate, said to me, "How's your book coming along?" and I told him, "Ironically, Tom, I am presently writing about General Haldane and I know that when you were a cadet, he was your "Tac" officer."

Tom then told me about a serious incident that occurred when he was the cadet in charge and they were returning by air from service with the 101st Airborne Division at Fort Campbell, and how then-Captain Haldane handled it 65 years ago. Tom said, "As a Cadet then entering my third year at West Point, I resolved to try to emulate his brand of leadership as I moved on—firm, quiet, efficient, and thoughtful. That is how he was—a born leader who no doubt became an even better leader as he progressed through his Army career."

Taps magazine is published at West Point and contains obituaries of graduates. This issue was from Spring/Summer 2010. His fascinating obituary ended this way: "General Robert Haldane's service and life exemplified the standards he held so dear. West Point: Duty, Honor, Country – First Infantry Division, The Big Red One: No mission too difficult, No sacrifice too great, Duty first."

In all that he achieved, General Haldane proved that he was truly a pillar of responsibility. I am proud to call him my friend.

CHAPTER 8

Fairness
DON HALDANE

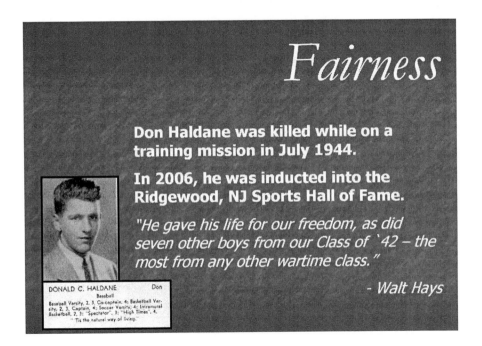

Fairness

Don Haldane was killed while on a training mission in July 1944.

In 2006, he was inducted into the Ridgewood, NJ Sports Hall of Fame.

"He gave his life for our freedom, as did seven other boys from our Class of '42 – the most from any other wartime class."

- Walt Hays

DONALD C. HALDANE   Don
Baseball
Baseball Varsity, 2, 3, Co-captain, 4; Basketball Varsity, 2, 3, Captain, 4; Soccer Varsity, 4; Intramural Basketball, 2, 3; "Spectator", 3; "High Times", 4.
" 'Tis the natural way of living."

on and I were in the same home room when we entered Ridgewood High in our sophomore year, and we both went out for football. Don was in position to make the varsity as fullback. He was six feet tall and weighed 175 pounds. I was six feet tall, weighed in at 110 pounds, and was on about the fourth team. Don broke his leg in a scrimmage, missed a couple months of school, and moved back to the class of 1942. I spent a lot of time with him, getting his school work to him while he was recuperating. We became very good friends and teammates.

Muhammad Ali said, "Champions aren't made in the gyms. Champions are made from something deep inside them. A desire, a dream, a vision." Great athletes become champions by leading; they play by the rules, take turns, and share. Be open minded, listen to others, don't blame others carelessly. Treat all people fairly, and when you can do that in four sports, you are a great player and a captain.

Don Haldane worked at a water well drilling company in the summer months, swinging sledge hammers that were used to sharpen bits, and carrying heavy pipes in order to build a strong, muscular body. We didn't have any weight-lifting programs in those years; you were on your own. He also had an excellent personality and was a very confident person. In addition to all of his athletic skills, he was a good student. Several years after the war ended, the athletic director at Ridgewood High School said at his retirement banquet that he had seen almost 2,500 young men go through his athletic program and that Don Haldane was the best all around athlete he had ever coached. Walt Hays and Bob Haldane teamed up to have Don enshrined in the Ridgewood High Athletic Hall of Fame.

Don was a very special athlete. As a high school senior, he was captain of the soccer, basketball, and baseball teams. His parents wouldn't let him play football because of the broken leg he incurred as a sophomore. He played shortstop, and besides being a great fielder with a strong arm, he could hit with power. Five major league teams were after him before he entered the Navy flight training program.

He was sent to preflight training at Chapel Hill, North Carolina. It was there that he starred at the division-one level playing football, and was one of the high scorers in the college ranks. In fact, Gene Goodreault, Boston College '41, who was coach at Chapel Hill, told Don that after the war, wherever he was coaching, Don would have a scholarship and a place on his team.

Incidentally, Gene was a pretty good judge of talent. His Bio reads: "One of the most outstanding ends in the history of New England college football." Gene was an All-East and All-American player on Boston College's 1940 Cotton Bowl and 1941 Sugar Bowl teams. Gene is enshrined in the National Football Foundation Hall of Fame.

DON HALDANE

After receiving his wings, Don was assigned to F6F Hellcats. One night flying to Jacksonville, Fla., in a flight of 12, he went down in a storm near Callahan, 35 miles west of Jacksonville. They were flying on instrument clearance with an understanding that they would need to be on clearance for five minutes, but they flew into thunderheads, heavy rain, and reduced visibility. Several of the flight became disoriented, only to regain control after losing considerable altitude. Don lost control and crashed.

A great career in baseball, marriage, and raising a family was lost forever, along with similar goals of millions of other young men in WWII. Walt Hays and I spent many evenings with Don's parents when we returned after the war. Don was an only child and their dreams had been shattered.

DON MCCULLOUGH

Don McCullough was an easy guy to know and a very good athlete. He played football, basketball, and baseball, all of them equally well. He wasn't too big in stature but very big in heart. He's the kind of guy that, if you were in a "fox hole" in combat, you would want him at your side.

Not everyone has the tools to be a superstar but given the right attitude, anything can be achieved. You might be smaller, you may not be quite as fast, and you might have to stay longer at practice and become a good teammate by improving one or two phases of your game. I believe that Don McCullough represents all the qualities of the "Fairness" pillar of "Its Character that Counts," just like our pal Don Haldane. He played by the rules, he took turns and shared. He was open-minded; he listened to others and treated others fairly. And in the greatest game of all, he would risk his life for a friend. He has "The Purple Heart" to prove it.

When I got to high school, Don and I became instant friends and, of course, we have continued that friendship all our lives. As I write, he is the only other member of our "Pillars of Character" group still living. He is the father of nine children. His wife Mary passed away many years ago, and at 91 years of age, he lives in Lake Winnipesaukee, in New Hampshire, where he proved his talent as an "impressionist painter." Several years ago he painted my portrait and I really appreciate it. We have been friends for 75 years.

When I told him I was writing this book, he sent me a "tattered picture" of Don Haldane in uniform. In 1943, when they were both home on leave, they traded pictures of themselves in uniform while visiting one of our favorite watering holes, "The Preakness Grill." Don had carried the picture for seventy years.

DON MCCULLOUGH

Don enlisted in the Marines in September of 1941. His family didn't have the resources to send him to college. We were not in the conflict yet but it was obvious that we would soon be involved. He was sent to boot camp at Parris Island, SC. When that was completed, he was selected to go to Sea School in Norfolk, Va. Only two out of the whole recruit company were picked to go. It was the only place that the Marine "blues" were issued.

On December 7, 1941, Don told me, he was walking guard duty under a battleship under construction when the officer of the day came looking for him to tell him that Japan had bombed Pearl Harbor. The next day they were looking for a Marine complement for the USS Washington and needed two more, so he shouted his name the loudest and was picked for the assignment. They went on a shakedown cruise in the Caribbean and then to Iceland to run the North Atlantic convoys to Russia. They lost their Admiral J W Wilcox overboard in rough seas. They chased the German battleship Von Terpitz all over the North Atlantic. Then they went through the Panama Canal to Hawaii and took part in the battle of Savo Island, where they sank several Japanese ships, including a Japanese battleship. As a result of the battle, their Admiral Lee was presented with the Navy Cross by Admiral Nimitz. They were also in the support group when "Doolittle's Raiders" flew off the carrier "Hornet" to bomb Tokyo.

After two years at sea, he was transferred back to the states and into the Sixth Marine Division. Then he went off to the invasion of Okinawa where he landed with George Company of the 22nd Marines. It was there that the famous war correspondent Ernie Pyle was killed by a Jap sniper. Don was wounded during the battle. In fact, the Marine medics were photographed by a New York newspaper carrying a marine across the battlefield. Back in NJ, Don's mother recognized that it was her son. She didn't even know where Don was, so she contacted the paper and they confirmed that it was he. He sent the picture to me but it was too old to reprint. He spent weeks in a Guam hospital recuperating.

Don McCullough is a great guy, a life-long friend, and a great American.

Okinawa was taken because it would be the "jump off" point for the invasion of Japan. The United States suffered 62,000 casualties and lost 768 airplanes. The Japanese had 95,000 military and 145,000 civilians killed. Most of these civilians were killed because they had been commandeered by the Japanese forces into the Army to fight the allies. The Japanese lost 7,830 planes, including 2,655 operational accidents. Navy and Marine Corps downed 3,047. Navy ships downed 409, and B29s destroyed 558 on the ground. The atomic bombs were dropped a couple weeks later and the Japanese surrendered.

CHAPTER 9

Caring
PAUL GRASSEY

PAUL GRASSEY　　　　Grass
Undecided
Football Squad, 2; Baseball, 2, 3; Varsity, 4;
Intramural Basketball, 3, 4; Y.M.C.A. Basketball
League, 4; A. A. Salesman, 4; Cast, Junior
Play; Willow Club, 4; Commencement Usher,
3; Publicity Committee, Senior Play.
"A man who is witty all day long."

ebruary 1946 was the start of a new life for me—a return to college at Lafayette in Easton, PA – where I had been earlier, during Air Corps training. A war had interrupted many of us who had begun college in 1941—called to serve in World War II. Some never made it back. As survivors we had a huge obligation to make sure that those who didn't return could rest assured that we would carry the torch for them and rebuild the country for which they had died. Only a few months had passed since life was as exciting as it can get, and now we had to regroup and prepare ourselves for the future.

After finishing my visit to the Dean's office to settle my academic program, I went down to the gym to visit Charley Gelbert, the school's baseball coach whom you will meet later in the book. He suggested that I play basketball on the JV to help me get in shape for the upcoming baseball season. While I was in his office, a young man named Bob Kiefer came in. He lived in Easton and had just returned from the service where he served in Italy as a B24 nose gunner in the 15th Air Force. He was there to play handball with Charley and Charley said, "Why don't you two play? Paul can get some gym clothes out of the equipment cage."

Bob and I had a great time; when we were finished, he asked where my room was and told me that he would pick me up that evening. He was driving a 1941 white Buick sedan. We hit a couple of college spots in Easton and while we were talking, I found out that he was a Phi Delt. I told him that when I had been an Aviation Cadet there, some guys from that fraternity stopped by and told me they had voted me in.

Bob and I became good friends. A few days later when we visited the Phi Delt house, I got a job as a waiter for free meals and was on a waiting list for a room there. Within a couple weeks I was living there with room and board and waiting tables.

Bob also informed me that he wouldn't have the car as often. His sister, whose husband had been killed in WWII, would soon be coming home from Palm Springs with her three-year-old son. She had been staying there with General Walker and his family. Incidentally, this general was an aide to General Patton and served on his staff with her husband. I wish to make note here that General Walker was later in charge during the Korean War and was killed in a jeep accident.

Several weeks later, I was shooting pool at the fraternity when Bob Kiefer came in with his three-year-old nephew. He sat him on the table and said, "Say hello to Paul." With that, Terry picked up a pool ball and threw it at me! Little did I know that 67 years later we would still be "son and dad." All it takes is for a dad to act like a dad and a son to act like a son. Whether it's his or hers or ours makes no difference as long as love is there to hold it all together.

While I was attending summer school at Lafayette a month or so later, Bob Kiefer was working as a waiter up in the Poconos. He called another friend of ours and suggested that we ride up with his sister to go to a dance at the resort. She drove Ted Uly and me up to the dance, and that is when I first met Jeanne Overton. Later I found out she was driving once a week to Allentown in the evening for "gold shots" for her rheumatoid arthritis. I told her I would drive with her so she wouldn't have to go alone.

Jeanne became the law librarian at Lafayette. I used to tell her to find some guy with a lot of money and remarry. She ignored the first part of that advice. We were married August 16th, 1947.

Terry was going to pre-school in the mornings with an English professor's daughter from across the street. We would take turns walking the two children home. The college professor's little girl would call her father "Dad," and one day Terry reached up, took my hand, and began calling me "Dad." How simple life can be!

It never entered my mind that we should change Terry's last name to mine. A lot of that had to do with the way "Pop" Dolan had handled the Van Tassel twins. They certainly felt he was their dad and they had a warm and loving relationship with him.

* * * * * * * * * * * * *

Major Terry Overton, Jeanne's husband, was a real war hero. He served in the ROTC at Lafayette College, and upon graduation was put on active duty. He made First Lieutenant in June of 1942. After desert training, he was named Aide-de-Camp to the newly activated IV Armored Corps in September 1942, and Captain in December 1942.

He then was sent on a special mission as A.D.C. to General Walton H. Walker in Africa, March – April, 1943, and returned to attend Command and General Staff School at Fort Leavenworth, Kansas. Captain Overton went overseas February 1944 and transferred to G3 [Operations] as Assistant Operations Officer for General Walker in

March, and was promoted to Major. The Major was on his way to a great military career when he was killed by a mortar shell during reconnaissance of a river crossing in France, September, 1944.

* * * * * * * * * * * * *

Things got quite busy for me the spring of 1948. The Lafayette baseball team began playing well and we made it to the College World Series by beating Seton Hall, Rutgers, Navy, and West Virginia in the Regionals.

We went on to play in the semi-finals at Winston Salem, NC. This was the first double elimination tournament in the College World Series format still being used today. We beat the University of Illinois and the University of North Carolina. Yale beat us and went on to play USC in the finals. USC then beat Yale to become the National Champions.

Incidentally, George Herbert Walker Bush played first base for Yale and was captain of the team. Many years later, our son Gary sent him the box score of one of the games I had played against him and he sent me a nice note. It's in my den.

Spring of 1948 I was interviewed by Burroughs Corporation and decided I would join them in New York City. We bought a house in my old hometown, Glen Rock, NJ. Terry continued in elementary school there, and Bob was born February 18, 1950.

I sold adding machines, calculators, cash registers and bookkeeping machines. I was paid $65.00 per week plus commission.

My first commission check was $750.00. I was very excited about it so I cashed the check and asked for small bills. That evening when I got home, I walked into the kitchen where Jeanne was preparing dinner and threw them up in the air. That's when I really got the urge to become a top salesman.

* * * * * * * * * * * * *

In fact, I became so good, the company sent me to the home office in Detroit to run the new exhibit center. My job was to demonstrate all our equipment to visitors from all over the world. I took a public speaking course at Wayne University and accepted all the speaking engagements that the Public Relations Department asked me to do. I even appeared on an early television show demonstrating the equipment.

We were in Detroit for eight years when I was asked to go to New York as a zone sales manager. This didn't make me very happy because I had my heart set on becoming a branch manager anywhere in the country. I had visited more than 140 branches while in Detroit and felt that a branch should be my first step, so I told management I didn't want to go. They finally asked the New York manager, Fred Kuhn, who had become a good friend of mine, to come in and talk to me. He said they wanted me to have the experience so that someday I could run New York.

December of 1958, Jeanne and I went down to New York and spent a few days there looking at houses in NJ. We saw a couple that we thought would fit our needs—then she went back to our home in Birmingham, Michigan. The first weekend after she had returned home, I received a phone call from some friends who told me Jeanne was in the hospital. They said she might have the flu and that my boys were staying with them.

I immediately headed home and went directly to Beaumont Hospital. Jeanne was very ill and passed away a few days later. The doctor told me they had misdiagnosed her illness—that when she had a D and C done in November, she had contracted staph disease. I got Terry out of high school and told him his mom had passed away, then went to elementary school and gave Bob the same bad news.

Jeanne had received her degree as a librarian at Simmons College in Boston, and had installed a library at Bob's elementary school. It was named the "Jeanne Grassey Library" in memory of the work she had done.

The boys and I had a sad train trip to Trenton NJ where Bob Kiefer picked us up. Jeanne was interred at the Southside Cemetery in

Easton, PA. Terry and Bob would stay with her mother and father at their home a block away from Lafayette.

I began working in New York City as a Zone Manager and had nine salesmen reporting to me. My territory was the garment area, upper Manhattan, and the South Bronx.

The Luckiest Day Of My Life

It wasn't the day that a remote voice on the radio in the center of the North Atlantic, in the middle of winter, at the point of no return, told my flight engineer and me where the booster pump switch was that would transfer the fuel from the "Tokyo" tanks to the main tanks in my B24. It wasn't the day that my gunners yelled over the intercom that they had hit an ME262 that was attacking us near Wesendorf, or the bad weather day when we missed the barrage balloon cables surrounding The Bay of Antwerp. My luckiest day was July 16th 1959.

This was the day I was invited by a friend of mine, Ed Miller, to go out on his boat in Freeport Long Island. Ed was the branch manager in Hempstead Long Island. His wife had passed away in December of 1958 and he had recently married an Air Force nurse from Mitchell Field. He and his wife had arranged for me to meet a captain, Nancy Steindl, who was a nurse at Mitchell Field.

When I arrived at the boat, everyone else was there plus one extra person—an attractive young Air Force nurse. She was not only easy to look at but she was easy to talk to. She was on orders to go to Seville, Spain in six weeks.

I did some water skiing and we all had lunch on the boat. Ed docked and we went into a bar to have a drink before I went back to the Officers Club at Mitchell Field. We were having a company dinner party there that evening.

There was some nice music playing on the juke box so I asked Nancy if she would care to dance. While dancing, I found out that she was 22 years old and that this would be her first trip overseas. I had carried a silver dollar in my wallet for good luck. On my last leave before going to the Eighth Air Force, I had a date with an old high school friend and she gave it to me for good luck. I gave it to Nancy and I said, "Here, take this. Maybe it will bring you good luck too."

Later at the Officer's Club as the party was getting underway, I thought to myself, I wonder if that nurse Nancy would come over if I called her. I didn't even know her last name, so I asked my friend Ed Miller who said "Steindl." I called her at the nurse's quarters and she accepted the invitation.

Later that evening we were sitting at the bar enjoying each other's company when one of my Burroughs friends, Charley Case, an ex-Navy pilot said to us, "Why don't you two get married?" I turned to Nancy and said "Would you like to get married?" and she said, "Yes, but how do I get out of going to Seville?" About the only way a nurse could get out of the Air Force was to have dependents under 18. I said, "I have two boys sixteen and nine." Nancy replied, "I'll have to talk to my head nurse Major McNulty."

We had to move fast, so we bought a house in Glen Rock. My friend Jack Duxbury owned a real estate agency and we put the deal together. We were married in the Chapel at Mitchell Field on August 22, 1959. Twenty four hours before Nancy was to leave from McGuire Air Force Base, she received a telegram from Washington telling her that she was discharged.

In addition to Terry and Bob, Nancy and I have two more children, Gary and Marianne. At this writing we have been married more than 53 years. She is Mom, Grandma, and Great Grandma to everyone. She is the one who makes it all work! She is the most caring person I have ever met. Was July 16, 1959 a great day or what? I love you Nancy!

* * * * * * * * * * * * *

I received this E mail from a friend today:

"Too often, we underestimate the power of a touch, a smile, a kind word, a listening ear, an honest compliment, or the smallest act of caring, all of which have the potential to turn a life around. People come into our lives for a reason, a season, or a lifetime! Embrace all equally!"

CHAPTER 10

Citizenship
HARRY AND ED
VAN TASSEL

EDWARD JOSEPH VAN TASSEL   Ed
Undecided
Basketball, 2, 3; Varsity, 4; Golf, 2, 3; Intramural Basketball, 2, 3, 4; "Spectator," 3; "High Times," 4; Publicity Committee, Senior Play.
"Like—but oh how different."

HAROLD GERARD VAN TASSEL   Har
Undecided
Basketball, 2, Varsity, 3, 4; Baseball, 2; Varsity, 3, 4; Chairman Hall and Corridors; Student Committee, 4; Student Council, 4; "Spectator," 3; "High Times," 4; Intramural Basketball, 2, 3, 4.
"Like—but oh how different."

have selected the Van Tassel twins as the pillars of "Citizenship". I first got to know them at Mt. Carmel Church in Ridgewood, NJ. We made our First Communion, and six years later we were confirmed. We attended Sunday school and by the time we entered high school we were very good friends.

Harry and Ed were an inseparable pair of twins. They did everything together and were almost identical. They grew up in Ridgewood. Their best friends were Don Haldane and Don McCullough. They played baseball and basketball together.

Harry was a good pitcher and, of course, I caught many games that he pitched in the American Legion League, high school, and semi-pros. One of his best efforts was a no-hit, no-run game in high school. The thing that carried him was a very fine knuckle ball.

Harry and Ed were excellent in basketball, and it was fun to watch them play in high school on the same team with the two Dons. Ed also played on the golf team and both of them were very good students. In addition, they were very popular and served on the student council and other high school organizations.

On Sunday afternoons during our senior year, several of us would be up at Mr. and Mrs. Dolan's house and she would make a wonderful lunch for us. Then we would go down to the school yard near their house and hit baseballs, shoot baskets, or throw a football around. Once in a while Mr. Dolan would let us have his Packard to ride around in; it was set up for a chauffeur with a window between the front and the back seats. We felt like "big shots."

In September of 1941, when I returned from Cuba, I met with Harry and Ed to find out what their plans were for college. Even though Pearl Harbor hadn't occurred yet, the United States was getting closer to being involved and our long-range plans were day-to-day.

I had started to work at Wright Aeronautical on the third shift (midnight to eight in the morning) in the cylinder head foundry. The twins were working at Botany Mills on the same shift. We decided to enter Bergen Jr. College night school and take some freshmen college courses from seven PM until eleven so we still could get to the third-shift jobs. Harry and Ed had purchased an old Dodge sedan and were kind enough to drive me back and forth to classes.

On December 7th, 1941, Pearl Harbor was attacked by the Japanese. The only thing that I wanted to do was to get enough credits for two years of college so I could become a pilot in the Army Air Corps.

March of 1942 was when their dad reenlisted from his service in WWI. Harry and Ed enlisted in the Army Air Corps and were assigned to the Ninth Air Force in England where they instructed paratroopers in jumping techniques. After D-Day they went to France with the Ninth Air Force cadre and both attained the rank of Captain. They served in the military for almost four years.

After discharge from the Army Air Corps, the Van Tassels entered Manhattan University on the GI Bill. Upon graduation they entered Notre Dame Law School. Following that, Ed began his own law practice in Ridgewood and Bergenfield, NJ, and Harry went to work for AT&T in Chicago.

Harry was Division Traffic Supervisor when he and Ed were admitted by Chief Justice Earl Warren to argue cases before the Supreme Court. Harry Van Tassel later became Comptroller of AT&T. To prove that if you live long enough, your life comes back to you, Howie Janotta, an old pal of mine from the Army Air Corps, flew Harry around the country as chief pilot for AT&T.

* * * * * * * * * * * *

Ed stayed with law and became Commissioner of both the Ridgewood Police Department and Fire Department. He was then appointed Superior Court Judge of Bergen County.

Ed was my son Gary's godfather. When Gary was attending Fordham Law School, he was required to do some summer work in a law office. I gave the Judge a call and he said, "Certainly, tell him to call me." After Gary completed his work in the office, Judge Van Tassel called and said, "This young man is great, he doesn't need any help."

Several years later, Ed passed away. My Ridgewood friends told me that more than a thousand people who couldn't get into Mt Carmel for the funeral service stood outside the church. He certainly was a pillar of citizenship.

* * * * * * * * * * * *

Ed Van Tassel in chambers and receiving an award in Ridgewood, NJ

Around the year 2003, Harry and his wife said they would like to visit The Mighty Eighth Air Force Museum in Savannah. Their granddaughter was attending the Savannah College of Art and Design and they had planned to visit her.

Harry was suffering from Parkinson's Disease and could only move around in a wheel chair. We had a very fine visit and I was able to show them around the Museum. They were accompanied by their daughter and granddaughter. That is when we arranged to get "Pop" Dolan's memorabilia from Walter Dolan's widow in Cooperstown, NY to the Mighty Eighth Air Force. Walter Dolan had maintained a "War Room" there for his dad. We have 120 items from Colonel Dolan's collection.

The last time I saw Harry before he passed away was at his condominium in Sarasota, Florida. We had attended the annual reunion of all classes from Ridgewood High School the day before.

Parkinson's disease had taken its toll and he was confined to his bed. I asked him what his and Ed's relationship was with "Pop." He proudly whispered to me, "When Ed and I would visit him in his New York office, he would introduce us as my sons, Ed and Harry. We were every bit as proud as he was." Harry too was a great brother, husband, father, grandfather and citizen. I am pleased to say that we were life-long friends.

SECTION THREE

In The Army Air Corps

Now we return to my personal story. I finally got my orders from the Army Air Corps in January of 1943 while in my second semester at V.P.I. I was to report in a few weeks. I said "so long" to Bob, who told me he would finish out the school year and then enlist. I headed back to Glen Rock and waited.

Those few weeks of waiting seemed like a century. When the orders finally arrived, I was very excited—I was on my way to attaining my goal of becoming a pilot. On the big day, I packed a small carry bag with a few items; went over to look at the fields where I had played football and baseball just a few years ago; then walked along the tracks up to the Erie Railroad Station. Here I was, 19 years old, all alone and going on an adventure with no clue how it would end.

I would spend over a year in training; make lifelong friends; lose several buddies in training and combat; and learn lessons which last to this day.

CHAPTER 11

Air Corps Training

It was at the Post Office in Newark, NJ that I first met the military and my fellow enlistees. There were about a hundred of us and we were formed in alphabetical order. I make a point of this because I soon would learn that most of my Army friends' names began with an E, F, G, H, I or J.

We then went to the Pennsylvania Railroad Station in Newark, got on a Pullman, and headed to "who knows where" for about three or four days. However, I made some good friends, like Bob Finehout, Pat Finnegan, Jack Gould, Johnnie Hanold, and Howie Janotta, while riding on the train, and we didn't split up until we arrived at the Classification Center in Nashville, Tenn., a few months later.

Training Begins

We finally arrived at our Basic Training Center in Keesler Field, Mississippi. After a couple days, we were issued uniforms and were allowed to send our filthy clothes home. After the war ended, my mom said she cried when they got there.

We lived in tents, ate out of mess kits, did plenty of marching with a drill sergeant, and had lots of physical training. If you weren't in good shape when you got there, you were when you left.

Then a little luck: we were about to be assigned to College Training Detachments around the country to begin our Air Cadet training; however, one of our New Jersey group knew the soldier handing out the assignments. He arranged to send about 75 of us to Lafayette College in Easton, PA.

I had never visited the "Old College on the Hill" even though I lived only 75 miles away. The dormitories were old except for Gates

Hall which was the newest. An old worn out dorm was Blair Hall, and there on the first floor across from the Quadrangle, Pat Finnegan, Jack Gould, Howie Janotta and I arranged to share a room.

After being ordered around by the cadet officers in the class ahead of us, we decided we would become the cadet officers in charge of our class before we were sent to our next assignment.

We were not allowed to play hard ball in the Air Corps but we could play fast-pitch softball. We put together the best team on the campus and the Lafayette team challenged us to a game. We beat them!

At Easton Airport with a Piper Cub

The Commander was an Army Air Corps pilot who lost his leg in the Philippines early in the war. He loved our team. He got us uniforms and we all became officers in the Cadet Corps. Our pitcher was Bill Dahl, who had a great fast ball. He became the Cadet Commander;

I was the catcher and became the Group Adjutant. Pat Finnegan had played centerfield for Fordham so he was our centerfielder. Jack Gould played second base for St Lawrence University so we had a second baseman; and Howie Janotta played basketball and baseball at LIU, so we had our third baseman. The last four were all Cadet Squadron Commanders and we now shared a big suite in Gates Hall. Captain Passadante took us around to play local colleges in Pennsylvania. This would be the last few weeks of fun and games because the real serious stuff would soon begin.

We had a lot of classroom studies and close order drill. We also got ten hours of flying time in Piper Cubs at the Easton Airport.

After about two and a half months at Lafayette, we were ready for the Classification Center in Nashville, Tenn. This is where you were given psychological, coordination, and depth-perception tests to determine if you were qualified for pilot training, navigator training, or bombardier training. It was the first opportunity to "wash out".

When the cadet class ahead of me was leaving, their Group Adjutant gave us a little pitch; and he impressed me with an anonymous poem that he had recited. I memorized it and have never forgotten it; it fits in so well with "Its Character That Counts"

I want to be able as the days go by
Always to look myself straight in the eye.
I don't want to stand with the setting sun
And hate myself for the things I've done.
But I want to go out with my head erect
And I want to deserve all men's respect.
For here in this struggle for fame and wealth
I want to be able to like myself.
Because I know what others may never know
And I see what others may never see;
So whatever happens I want to be
Self-respecting and conscience free.

The poem has stayed with me my whole life. It describes "Character" as well as any words I have ever seen. Even today, as I make "power point presentations" to many different audiences, I always finish with those words. It has been an inspiration to me.

That Group Adjutant impressed me with his overall performance as well. His bearing was very military and he was very confident of his own ability. At the College Training Detachment level, the Group Adjutant was the cadet in charge. He gave all the orders whenever the Group marched. In a parade, he was the one who shouted the commands; and it was he who assigned cadets to guard duty every evening and announced the orders of the day at the first formation in the morning. I decided I wanted that assignment and I won it.

(Little did I know at this time that I would graduate from Lafayette after the war.)

The Classification Center

We arrived in Nashville to find a very busy base with cadets arriving from many College Training detachments throughout the east coast. We would probably be there for six weeks. The barracks were quite old and larger than we had seen before. We did a lot of physical training, along with the classification tests.

While at Lafayette, I found out I was a pretty good long-distance runner. I never had good sprint speed but I enjoyed cross country and we did a lot of it in Nashville.

I volunteered for night "KP" because the mess sergeant and I got along pretty well; and I could eat like a king. I also volunteered at the butcher shop and managed to come back to the barracks with a few steaks, which we never saw in our mess hall. My pals Finnegan, Janotta and I would cook them on the stove that heated the barracks. Even with all the exercise I was getting, my weight went from 175 to 225, and I have maintained the same weight for more than 70 years.

When we received our classifications, Janotta and I were going to pilot training; Finnegan was going to bombardier training. Pat was from Hoboken, NJ; and, even though he had graduated from Fordham and was a terrific athlete, he never had a driver's license nor had he even driven a car when he entered the service. When he was getting his 10 hours flight training—his first ride in an airplane—his instructor that day told him to "let go of the stick; you're holding it too tight." Pat told him, "Calm down, I'll put this thing in the hangar for you." I think that's one of the reasons he was classified as a bombardier.

Our next stop was pre-flight training at Maxwell Field, Alabama. Once again, we left for this new challenge and the good news was, we were only a month and a half away from Primary Flight training.

Preflight Training

John Hanold, Howie Janotta, and me at Maxwell Field

Maxwell Field was the most "storied" preflight school in the country. The challenges were many and we looked forward to getting this phase over and moving on to actually fly airplanes.

First of all, we were required to take part in a heavy schedule of physical training. We had to run the "Burma Road" almost every other day. It was part of our cross-country running and it was a real test of one's stamina and strength. We did a lot of calisthenics and close-order drill. We shot 45s, Carbines, and skeet with twelve gauge shot-guns.

Our classroom study was very serious as well. Some of the courses were aircraft recognition, Morse Code [in both sound and flashing lights], physics, mathematics, and map reading.

We had to go into a pressure chamber that simulated 35,000 feet. When a red light went on, we had to don oxygen masks. With those masks, we were required to enter a small building that soon filled with tear gas. This, of course, was to give us confidence and to let us know that we could survive under those conditions.

Physical exams were frequent. Meanwhile, I discovered that when the dentist filled 12 of my teeth at Nashville, he didn't do a very good job. I had problems in the pressure chamber. My decision was to do nothing about it because I didn't want to lose class time and run the risk of getting left behind.

During our stay at Maxwell we had a two-hand touch football league [we were not allowed to play tackle football]. One Sunday we had the championship game. Here were some of the players: Bob Cifers, who played at the University of Tennessee and after the war for the Pittsburgh Steelers. Russ Coates, a good friend of mine who had played for the University of Miami and the Washington Redskins. Russ was a full-blooded American Indian and a very talented athlete. Clint Casselberry, All-American quarterback as a freshman at Georgia Tech. Clint was later killed in combat. A cadet named Childress from Vanderbilt. I remember his name because we rode in the same ambulance to the base hospital. He had a knee injury and I received 10 stitches over my right eyebrow. I still carry the scar.

Serving in the Army Air Corps during World War II, you soon found out it didn't matter where you came from, what side of the tracks you lived on, or whether you were rich or famous. It didn't matter who you were before you got into the service. It was whether you could do the job or not.

All that mattered was if you had the "Character" to get to your ultimate goal, a pilot in the Army Air Corps. Here's a poem that says it all.

The Guy In The Glass
By Dale Wimbrow

When you get what you want in your struggle for pelf,
And the world makes you king for a day,
Then go to the mirror and look at yourself,
And see what that guy has to say.

For it isn't your Father, or Mother, or Wife,
Whose judgment upon you must pass.
The feller whose verdict counts most in your life
Is the guy staring back from the glass.

He's the feller to please, never mind all the rest,
For he's with you clear up to the end,
And you've passed your most dangerous difficult test
If the guy in the glass is your friend.

You may be like Jack Horner and "chisel" a plum,
And think you're a wonderful guy,
But the man in the glass says you're only a bum
If you can't look him straight in the eye.

You can fool the whole world down the pathway of years,
And get pats on the back as you pass,
But your final reward will be heartaches and tears
If you've cheated the guy in the glass.

On To Primary Training

Most of the Primary schools were managed by civilians; and Helena, Arkansas was one of them. It had an Army Air Corps Major and a staff of Army Air Corps officers in charge, but all the instructors were civilians and each had 1000-or-more hours of flying time. The Major's staff was there to see that the school was following Air Corps protocol, to give the cadets check rides, and to teach Link Trainer and required classes.

The facility was very nice compared with Army bases and the food was great. My instructor's name was Burnett, a very nice guy with plenty of patience. The planes at this base were PT19s, a single-engine, low-wing plane with two open cockpits. The one up front was for the instructor and the one behind for the student. After we soloed, we could fly in the front seat.

PT19

Finally, we were learning to fly and the training was very intense. We spent the first six or seven hours with our instructors learning to fly patterns and turns, then to climb to about 3,000 feet and do some spins and stalls from which you learned to recover, before shooting takeoffs and landings. Then the big day came when the instructor said, "OK you're ready to go! Taxi over to that marker and let me out. Make three take-offs and three landings and then come back and pick me up."

Wow, what a feeling! Each take-off and landing got easier as your confidence grew. However, when I taxied over to pick up Burnett, one of my wheels got stuck in the mud and we had to get the plane pulled out. The instructor said, "You did fine, but you also came in too low over the power lines. That means that you will have to go to 'Night Court' next week." My sentence was 20 tours carrying a rifle at the parade ground.

When we arrived at Primary training, all 176 of us were named "Dodos." We had to wear our flight goggles hanging over the back of our necks when we were on the ground. After we soloed, we were allowed to wear them the normal way - over our forehead. We were then the envy of all the other cadets who were still "Dodos."

It's very ironic, but my brother "Hank" was there to greet me when I landed after my three solo flights. He made a surprise visit from the Memphis Air Station. It was great to see him but even more exciting to tell him that I had just soloed.

Let me tell you what happened during my session at "Night Court". I was sitting next to a cadet who was also waiting for his punishment because of a rules violation. His name was "Rosey" Rosenberg from Newark NJ. The major in charge of the court asked him to stand and said, "Cadet Rosenberg, it is my understanding that you became lost while you were flying a routine assignment last week; you ran low on fuel and had to make a forced landing. However, you picked out a nice field, made a nice landing, called us, and after refueling, returned safely to the base. Therefore, we won't give you any tours. Next case."

After the court closed and I gave him my congratulations, he said, "Let me tell you what really happened. I was up getting some flying time and I decided to fly over and see what the Mississippi River looked like. I became lost and was getting low on fuel. I decided that I better make a forced landing. I picked out a nice field and went in to land, over-shot and luckily landed without hitting a rock or tree."

When he got out of the plane and looked around, he realized it was a miracle he didn't hit anything. Rocks and trees were all over the place. The farmer who owned the property came out and when "Rosie" told him his predicament, the farmer called some of his neighbors. They got a tractor and moved the plane into the nice field on the other side of the fence. Then he called the air base. They came out with gasoline and he flew back to the main field and received their congratulations.

My friend "Cactus" Coates was in a very serious incident during primary training. After completing our morning flight assignment, he said, "Hey Paul, you have to hear what just happened to me. I climbed to 3,000 feet and decided to practice recovering from a spin. I got into the spin OK and when I tried to recover, I couldn't get out until I was just a few feet from the ground. I was really frightened and thought I had done something wrong during the recovery procedure. I went up again; put the plane into the spin, and the same thing happened. I decided I'd better land and check with the instructor. He had the ground crew check my plane and found that one of the ailerons wasn't functioning properly."

"Cactus" wouldn't be so lucky in a B24 seven months later at the Charleston, SC Replacement Training Unit. The statistics show that 54,000 trainees were killed in the U.S.A. trying to become pilots in World War II.

From our primary flight school publication, *Primememories*,

A "Typical day", At the Fifty Ninth Army Air Force Flying Training Detachment:

0530 begins the official day whereupon we reluctantly dress and fallout, shivering in the cold night air, for roll call. Chow quickly follows which brightens things. Room orderlies by this time are pushing us to clean and straighten our section of the barracks.

At 0700 we head for the flight line where a "Pep talk" is given by the squadron commander and dispatcher. Chutes are picked up and you start hunting for your ship.

"Switch off, controls unlocked, brakes set, gas on fuller tank, pressure up, throttle pumped and cracked, on left mag." Forms are filled out and finally you are off into the "Wild Blue Yonder." At 1230 all the "Hot Pilots" are "sweating out" another chow line, namely dinner, and by the next hour, ground school has started. After two hours of this, you rush to your room for a quick change—then drilling.

"Physical Torture" starts with a quick half-mile sprint, followed by calisthenics and the obstacle course, with games coming last on the day's program.

After a good hot shower comes "Mail Call." Anything is welcome even if it's only a post card, though we would rather have a "Sugar" report from the one-and-only.

We stand retreat, a short but impressive ceremony, at 1830, 6:30 P.M. to civilians, at which time the flag is lowered, and orders of the day are read; then off to supper. From 2000 to 2130 you study or write letters. After a fast job on your teeth and possibly a second shower, you hit the sack. Another day has passed and we are one day nearer graduation and final Victory!

Finally, after 65 hours flying time and 5 hours of instrument time, we are ready for the BT13 and Basic Flying School. The experience will be a real test. I found out that I am headed for Greenville, Mississippi, for that episode.

Basic Flying School

BT13

Greenville, Mississippi was a nice little town located on the banks of the "Grand Old River." The airbase was quite large and surrounded by a few auxiliary fields. We were back in the Army again and away from that relatively soft civilian Primary base.

The BT13, the "Vultee Vibrator", was the basic trainer most widely used by the Army Air Corps during WWII. It represented the second of three stages of pilot flight training. It was considerably heavier and more powerful than the Primary Training Airplanes and considerably more complex.

We used two-way radios for communication. It had operating landing flaps and a variable pitch propeller. It used a Pratt and Whitney R-985 engine. The BT13 had two seats covered by a canopy. The instructor sat in the front seat and the student behind him; when we flew alone we operated out of the front seat. It was here I met and flew with a man who had a tremendous influence on me: my instructor, Lt. Frink.

Lt. Frink wasn't allowed to be an Air Force officer because he disobeyed flight regulations and was caught flying under bridges on the Mississippi River. Frink was a very tough man and a super pilot. He identified me as a very "cocky" guy who needed to be cut down to size; and in retrospect, he read it right.

After about four hours of flight training time in a BT13, he flew me over to an auxiliary field for an introduction to night flying. I shot a few landings with him and he really "ate me out" for coming in too low over the power lines. Then he climbed out of the cockpit and said "Take the plane back to the main base." I asked, "Are you going with me?" He replied, "Do you think I'm nuts? I wouldn't ride with you! I'm going back with somebody else." So there I was flying solo for the first time in a BT13 at one o'clock in the morning. I made a nice landing at the main base.

The next morning he gave me an order to go the same auxiliary field and said, "I'll meet you there." When he arrived, he told me to put my chute on and stand on a bench until he told me to get down. Then he said, "I want all your friends to see you, and when they ask you why you're doing this, tell them that you stupidly flew too low over the power lines last night."

This wasn't the only discipline he threw at me. He would take me up over the Mississippi and do slow rolls, snaprolls, loops, and immelmans. Then he'd put the plane into a spin and yell, "Get it out you #@$&%." And all the time, he made me keep the canopy closed to see if he could make me sick.

One day I was scheduled for a check ride, and as I walked out of the operations room he yelled at me "Don't walk into any props, bubble brains!."

That same day I was scheduled for a session in a BT14. When I arrived at the plane my instrument flying instructor, a Second Lieutenant, said to me, "Stop worrying, Paul. For some reason Frink wants you to think you're about to get washed out every time you go up in a plane. You're doing fine."

Towards the end of Basic Flight Training, we learned formation flying. Lt. Frink would take me and another cadet whom we called "Pappy" (he was 26 years old) to fly on each of his wings. It was summertime and I can still see Frink today as he would fly right into a thunderhead to see if we could stay with him. He'd come out the other side of the cloud with his canopy open and a big grin on his face, hoping he had lost us.

When we landed he would say, "You two are lousy formation pilots! If you go to England you'll have to fly through 20,000 feet of clouds in formation, so you'd better get it right!"

Preparing to solo in a BT13

On our way to Advanced Flight School in Stuttgart, Arkansas, "Pappy" Hall told me he was in the operations room and overheard

Lt. Frink telling his next class of trainees that they would never be able to fly formation as well as the two cadets he just was flying with--Grassey and Hall. I really believe Lt. Frink saved my life!

By the time we had completed Primary and Basic Flight Training, we had about 135 hours of flight time and more than 40 percent of our class had "washed out." That was the dreaded thought that raced through our minds as we looked toward our ultimate goal of getting those silver wings. The sad thing was that a few of the cadets in each class were killed in accidents. However, we had become a lot more confident about our capability as we moved on to Advanced Flight Training, but also were aware that we still had a lot to learn. As the saying goes, "There are old pilots and there are bold pilots, but there are no old, bold pilots."

Twin Engine Advanced Training

Getting to Advanced was a huge step for us in our quest for those silver wings. Twin engine advanced meant that when we finished our 75 hours of flight training, link training, and classroom work, we would be ready to fly some type of multi-engine plane and maybe get to combat. We arrived at the air base in Stugart, Arkansas and were assigned to our barracks. I was still with three other guys I had been with since the train ride from Newark—Bob Finehout, Cactus Coates, and Bill Johnson. It was August and we had upper and lower bunk beds covered with mosquito netting, nothing fancy. We would be spending most of our time flying or at the flight line.

Our airplane was a two-seat arrangement, side by side, pilot and copilot. Your flying partner would be either another cadet or your instructor. The plane was an AT10 made out of plywood, manufactured by Beech Air Craft out of Wichita, Kansas. It was powered by two Lycoming engines. My instructor was Captain Fanning, an Air Force officer who proved to be a very good teacher. We did a lot of cross country flying, navigational training, formation flying, night flying, and night formation.

AT10

Night formation was difficult. You had to fly in very tight formation which could cause "vertigo" if you weren't careful. I'll never forget one night when another cadet and I took off to fly on our instructor's wing. Right after takeoff, the red fuel-pressure warning light went on, so I radioed the instructor and told him. The Captain said, "If its bothering you, take the bulb out"; so I did.

Another evening while shooting night landings at an auxiliary field with no landing lights on (we called them "blackout" landings: only little green lights outlined the blacktop runway), one of the brakes felt as if it were sticking. I radioed the control tower where a couple of instructors were monitoring the take-offs and landings and told them about the problem. Incidentally, we were doing these take-offs and landings solo. They told me to fly the plane back to the air base so I followed orders.

When I landed the plane it spun around into the infield. When I walked into the training squadron building, the Army Air Corps officer in charge said he had a call from the tower. They told him I had ground-looped the AT10 and I should wait for the report from maintenance. A few minutes later he came out of his office and said "Paul, you're off the hook; it wasn't your fault, there was grease on the brake drum."

The last thing we had to do at this level was earn an instrument card. This was not easy. We had green glass as a windshield and wore red celluloid goggles. You could see only the instrument panel. The test was to fly an instrument landing let-down pattern for one of the runways three times, each time touch down, then return to the let-down pattern without a flaw. They gave you three tries to get it right, and some of the cadets couldn't get it done. What a tough place to "wash out"—at the very end of your flight training. Fortunately, I didn't have a problem and we received our wings at a ceremony and were ready for the next assignment.

CHAPTER 12

The Real Thing

Introduction to the B24

After graduating from Advanced, we were given a 10-day leave; and my orders were to report to Harlingen, Texas when the leave ended. It took two days and two nights to get to Glen Rock, and three nights and two days to get to Harlingen. Bob Finehout, who lived in Plainfield, NJ and I had the same orders, so we met in New York's Penn Station and took the long train ride to the Harlingen air base.

Harlingen was actually an Air Force gunnery school and the gunners were trained by shooting out of B24s. Pilots sent there were required to get 35 hours of flying time in the B24; then were sent to become co-pilots on their assigned crew.

My first day on the flight line, I was assigned to a plane, and when I climbed into the cockpit, I thought to myself, "Wow, this is some airplane!" The instrument panel was very impressive and the pilot explained what most of the instruments were used for. The four Pratt and Whitney engines looked and sounded very powerful.

We took off and flew around for a couple hours, and I got to fly the "Liberator" most of the time we were in the air. Regardless of rumors one might have heard, the B24 was a smooth flying plane. Those four R1830 Pratt and Whitney engines pulled 1600 horsepower each.

A couple days later, I had an opportunity to get another two hours flying time. After we landed, I walked into the operations office and they handed me an envelope with new orders. Eight others and I were to leave immediately for Westover Field, Mass. to join our flight crews. We had been at Harlingen 10 days, our flying time was "padded," and away we went to prepare for combat.

Instrument Panel on a B24

I was very happy to be on my way and so were the rest of the "10-day wonders." The next day we were to go over land to Brownsville, Texas; then catch an Eastern airliner to Westover, Mass.

We left Harlingen in two cabs and had to change cabs when we crossed into the next county on our way to Brownsville. After changing cabs, I discovered I had left my briefcase with all my personnel records in the cab that was now heading for Harlingen. I was in the front seat and yelled at the Mexican driver to turn around and catch the other cab. He shouted that he couldn't drive in the other county, so I put my foot on the top of his and floored the accelerator. It took us about five miles but we caught up and I had the brief case back in my hands. The driver wasn't very happy with me but I saved myself from a bad situation.

To make matters worse, a very bad storm had begun to build up by the time we reached Brownsville. Our plane was to leave at midnight so the nine of us checked into a hotel; got the largest room, and equipped it with beer. We left for a café for dinner. It was eerie—

there was no one outside but us and the café was empty. After we ate, we went back to the hotel and finished the beer. We concluded there was a hurricane on the way.

We caught a couple of cabs and went to the airport. It was a tiny terminal and mobbed with people who were waiting for our highest-priority military seats. The attendants were about to give them away as we arrived, but they quickly put us on the plane, a DC2 which only held about 20 passengers. It took about 12 stops and 15 hours to get to Westover Field.

Preparation For Combat

When we walked into the" Ready Room", there was a First Lieutenant looking for me. He said, "Hi Paul, I'm Jim Hey." We shook hands and became life-long friends. The last time I called him, I knew he was very ill with cancer, but I wanted him to be at the opening of the Mighty Eighth Museum in Savannah. I told him I was going to drive up to Rockport, Illinois, and drive him back for the opening. He said, "I can't do it 'Gringo.' Goodbye, I love you." I said, "Goodbye 'Fat Foe,' I love you too."

Those two nick-names were the ones we used to communicate with each other on the intercom or the radio. Jim was 26 years old (another oldster!) and had served in the Field Artillery before he transferred to the Army Air Corps. We rounded up the rest of our crew, and the next morning we left by train for Charleston, SC and the B24 Replacement Training Unit which would prepare us for combat. I didn't tell him that I had only four hours flying time in the "Liberator."

Charleston was a very large air base and well equipped with flight training equipment. I spent time with our navigator in the "silo" that was used for training on the latest navigational equipment, and with the bombardier in his training area to learn how to use the Norden bomb sight. We had to take down the gasoline lines on an engine and put them back together.

Jim Hey was not only an excellent pilot but he was a great instructor. In a few weeks he had me shooting takeoffs and landings, and it wasn't long before we had gained the reputation of being excellent formation pilots. Frink had convinced me in Basic that the name of the game was to fly tight formation and that's what I loved to do. In fact, when reading comparisons with the B17, it said the B24 was more difficult to fly in formation.

Jim and I didn't buy that. We did a great deal of night flying and did night camera bombing of Atlanta, Birmingham, Savannah and Mobile. One night we flew to two or three of these cities and our radio went out. Then on the way back to Charleston the visibility became poor. To make matters worse, our navigator got lost and the only thing we could do was to fly to the coast and look for the air base. We flew up and down the beach but couldn't find Charleston; and we were getting low on fuel. Finally we spotted some runway lights. We had the radio operator flashing SOS out of the waist window as we circled the field to check on the runway to see if it was long enough. The tower turned on all the runway lights as we circled and we landed safely. We taxied up to the hangars and opened the bombay doors. A maintenance man popped his head in. I said to Preston Plumb, our navigator, "Preston, ask him where we are?" The maintenance man said "Wilmington." Preston asked, "Wilmington, Delaware?" The man said, "No, Wilmington, NC. This is a Navy Base!" We refueled, called the Charleston base, and told them we would fly the light line back to our base, which we did.

About a week later my pal "Cactus" Coates was flying co-pilot on a B24 that took off from Charleston early one morning flying west out of the sun. A P47 flying east out of Walterboro hit them head-on and all were killed. I felt very sad for everyone but very sad about my friend. We had been together for a long time.

We flew some gunnery ranges at low level near Parris Island to give our gunners an opportunity to practice shooting at ground targets. We also dropped practice bombs on the beaches near Charleston. Just before we received our orders for England and the Mighty Eighth, we were sent to Cuba and Batista Field. We did some practice bombing outside of Havana the afternoon we arrived. The next day we loaded up the bomb bay with enough cases of duty-free and tax-free alcoholic beverages to supply the officers club at Charleston for the next year. It was so tough to get off the runway, I thought that we must have a supply for two years. I must admit this trip to Cuba was much different from my trip in June of 1941.

Our B24 Crew before departure

Ready For Flight To England

We received our orders early in December. Those of us on our way to England boarded a Pullman in Charleston on a Thursday afternoon and arrived at Mitchell Field, Long Island late Friday afternoon. Our plane would be ready for a four-hour check-out ride Saturday morning, with still enough time for me to lead a contingent to Manhattan on Friday night.

I took Peck Burkhardt, Bob Finehout, and Ed Beebe to the Schweinlers' Riverside Drive apartment and we had an impromptu "going away party." Mrs Schweinler was once again a gracious hostess along with her daughters Marie and Helen who all wished us good luck. Louise was away and, of course, still very down since Don Haldane, her fiancé, had been killed in his F6F crash.

My pals and I went to the subway and returned to Mitchell Field on the Long Island Railroad. When we arrived at the BOQ, there were orders on the bulletin board advising which plane we were to take up in the morning for a four-hour flight around Long Island. That would be the plane that we were to take overseas Monday AM.

It had snowed Friday afternoon and evening on Long Island. The runway was pretty short and there were piles of snow and ice around them when we took off. The plane had only six hours on it, which is the time it took to fly from Willow Run to New York.

Everything appeared to be working well during our shake-down flight. When it became time to land, I called the tower and who told us there had been a change in wind direction and we were to land on an even shorter runway and to be careful because it had some icy spots. The landing was ok; but when I hit the brakes, we skidded into a pile of ice and snow and the nose wheel broke. It looked like we would have to wait a couple weeks for another B24.

Saturday afternoon, I got a couple of my friends and rented a car. I called Mom and Dad and told them I would be home for dinner with two friends. We sure looked forward to some great home cooking by Mom Grassey. She didn't disappoint us! We had a great pot roast and a wonderful visit. I told my parents it might be a couple weeks until we could get another plane.

When we arrived back at Mitchell Field, there was a notice on the bulletin board that they had another B24 for us and we were scheduled for a test ride Sunday morning.

This time, even though we were supposed to stay over Long Island, I decided that we should fly over to Glen Rock and buzz my home a couple times. Down Doremus Avenue we flew, just over the tree tops, then back to Long Island for the rest of the shake-down cruise, landing at Mitchell Field with no more incidents. I called Mom and told her that I wouldn't be home for a while. She asked, "Was that you who flew over the house this morning?" I didn't know who might be monitoring phone calls so I just said, "So long Mom."

The Night God Winked At Me

In the military, it would probably be more fitting to say "the times" God winked at me. One thing for sure is that you will never know how you are going to react until you are faced with a life or death situation.

Our first stop for refueling was Bangor, Maine at Dow Field. Even before we landed, the snow had begun to fall and we had to tie down the plane because they expected about two feet, accompanied by heavy winds. It was about a week before we could leave for Goose Bay, Labrador.

We were restricted to the base for security reasons. However, I convinced the Special Services officer that the crews that were heading for combat had very low morale, and we should have some coeds at the University of Maine come to the base the next evening for a dance. He agreed. Of course, I fell in love with Jacqui, and when we finally took off for Goose Bay, four of the B 24s at my suggestion buzzed the University of Maine to say farewell. Later on, Jacqui sent me a V Mail saying we had broken a couple of windows at the University. Gosh, I wish I could remember her last name.

The flight to Goose Bay was routine. After about five hours, we arrived there to be briefed for our trip to Valley Wales, England. There were about 40 feet of snow piled up along the sides of the runways, and we stepped out into 35-below- zero temperatures.

We were to be at the base about three days. There was an Officers' Quarters, a Non-Com barracks, a mess hall, and a briefing facility. When you walked to each location there was nothing but snow and ice piled 20 feet high on each side of the road.

We spent many hours learning about the base in Greenland, which was located on a glacier at the dead end of a fjord. The briefing officer made you look at a rock formation until you had it implanted in your mind. If the ceiling was below 8,000 feet when landing, you were to make a sharp left turn at that exact location to reach the runway at the end of the fjord – any farther and there was no way out.

Late in the afternoon on the fourth day we were summoned to the briefing room. The briefing officer told us a 100 mile-per-hour tail wind was expected that night and we were to skip Greenland and fly directly across the North Atlantic to Valley Wales riding the tail wind.

The B24 with "Tokyo Tanks" [extra wing tanks] had a range of twelve and one-half hours – there was no room for error. Sixteen B24s were to make the trip. After a briefing with our navigator, we took a nap; bundled up in our flight gear, and then were taken by truck to our plane.

Our last minute instructions were to taxi to our takeoff runway, and after we ran up the engines, fuel trucks would be there to top off the main tanks; however, we couldn't lock the brakes because they would freeze. Heavily loaded, we used the whole runway to take off and turned to our heading for England.

After flying at about 12,000 feet for seven hours, my flight engineer, Jack Tardieu came up to the cockpit and said ,"I can't transfer the fuel from the "Tokyo" tanks to the main tanks." I said, "We should have done that after take-off and reaching our cruising altitude. We are now at the point of no return, six hours of fuel left, seven hours from Goose Bay, seven hours from Iceland, and seven hours from England."

We had no previous experience with this latest M model B24, and ditching in the North Atlantic was not an option. Our only option was to see if we could make radio contact with another B24 crew that might be flying the same model on this flight to England.

We radioed our call letters for about 15 minutes with no answer until suddenly a voice said, "We had the same problem. There is a booster pump behind the forward cabin door to the bomb bay. It needs to be in the 'on' position." Twenty minutes later Jack came to me and said, "The fuel is transferring!" Was that a "wink" from the Good Lord or what?

However, the night wasn't over. An hour or so later the number three engine began to lose manifold pressure; it remained at 14 inches. If it went to 12 inches, it would create a drag and we would have to feather the prop. The hydraulic system is powered by that engine and is needed to raise and lower the wheels and to operate flaps and brakes.

We thought that altitude might be the answer; but as we climbed, we started to lose manifold pressure on the number four engine—which told us it was a supercharger problem, so we went down to 10,000 feet and got the engines back to normal.

After about eleven and a half hours and with the morning sun shining brightly, we looked down through a light cloud cover and saw the word "EIRE"! What a wonderful sight! As we crossed the Irish Sea, we realized we were almost out of fuel. Should we land at Belfast or try to reach the Valley Air Base? Landing in Ireland would put the plane and possibly the crew out of the war, since Ireland held neutral status. Guts it! We went on to Wales, making a hot landing with only fifteen minutes of fuel left. Thank You God! But we're afraid that we are going to need you again in the near future.

* * * * * * * * * * * *

Sixty years later, thanks to research done by our flight engineer's daughter, I found out that 4 of the 16 B24s that left from Goose Bay that night were lost. Our trip to join the Mighty 8th Air Force had begun at Mitchell Field, Long Island, NY, just two miles from where Lindbergh took off on his famous trip. Little did we know that "Lindy" had a better chance of making it across the North Atlantic than we did.

Bungay, England

The purpose of Valley Wales Air Base was to take over the B24s or the B17s that arrived from United States and prepare them for combat. The rubber de-icer boots would be taken off the leading edge of the wings and replaced with metal, because the sky would get filled with flak and 50-caliber shell casings could cause damage to the rubber boots. The gun turrets would be prepared for action, and any mechanical problems that were encountered on the way over would be repaired. For example, the electronic superchargers on our number three and four engines needed to be repaired or replaced. Then the planes would be flown to the bases to which they were assigned. The crews would get food and a good night's rest after the long cold flight to England.

We were ordered to the 446BG, Bungay, England, the 704th Squadron.

We were taken by train to our Air Base and assigned to a barracks that was more like a hut. I think the picture below tells the story best about our new home and and our new pals.

We had another touch of good luck. The plane we had flown over from Mitchell Field was sent to Bungay from Valley Wales. We asked for it and the Group CO approved it. Our twin tails would be marked "X for Xray." Our crew chief, Ossie Osborne, suggested we name it "Lady Luck 2." After our crew agreed, we asked him what happened to "Lady Luck!" He said it had finished 25 missions and the crew was asked to fly five more, which it did successfully. But before returning to the states, the pilot, co-pilot and flight engineer were asked to fly some troops on special orders to another base in England. The pilot, against better judgment, tried to land in bad weather, the plane crashed, and all aboard were killed. We decided that the Lady Luck name and nose art would stay – the 25 missions were very impressive!

CHAPTER 13

On Mission

Preparation*

We had more than 100 air bases throughout East Anglia. A base housed about 2,500 men. They included the men who flew the planes and the ground personnel who serviced the planes or supported air operations. A group had about 40 planes made up of four squadrons.

A heavy bomber (B17 Fortress and B24 Liberator) crew was composed of 10 men. There were four officers and six enlisted men: The pilot, co-pilot, navigator, bombardier, radio operator, flight engineer, and waist, top, tail, and ball-turret gunners. Later on in the war when nose turrets were installed, the nose gunners would drop the bombs after seeing smoke bombs from the squadron lead ship. There were bombardiers only in the lead and deputy-lead planes. The crews were all ordinary young men – teenagers and men in their early twenties—doing extraordinary things under unimaginable conditions.

Every night when the mission was on, each of us would get a chance to be CQ (Charge of Quarters). Our job was to audit the "V mails" to make sure that no security rules were broken; and to sound the wake-up call to our huts. The CQ would go to each hut in the squadron and call out the names of the crews flying, making sure they were awake. "Okay guys, briefing at 0300."

Usually it was bitter cold because the fire in the single stove in the hut had gone out, and it was too cold to get out of the sack and start it. Then down to the latrine and wash and shave. If you didn't shave, the oxygen mask wouldn't fit snugly and your face might get frostbite. Then to the mess hall—most of the time, powdered eggs and coffee—and on to the briefing.

In the briefing rooms, a curtain covered the map of Europe. When it was uncovered, a long red ribbon stretched from the base to the target. If it was a deep penetration, there would be groans. A "milk run" brought sighs of relief. The intelligence officer explained the target, the route in and out, enemy aircraft that we might meet, where we could expect flak, and where we would see friendly fighter cover.

Our other enemy was weather. The Weather Officer would give us a forecast, in and out. The weather over the continent was hard to predict because of the effect from the Atlantic Ocean and the North Sea. The Chaplains gave their blessings—there weren't too many non-believers in combat. Trucks took us to the hard stand where the plane was being checked by the crew chief and his men. Then we boarded the plane.

If the mission was a short run, we were given one candy bar; if it were medium length—maybe six or seven hours, we would get two candy bars; and over 10 hours we would get three candy bars.

As the air war progressed, so did the clothing for combat. We wore woolen long johns, and most of us wore an electrically heated suit. Then flying coveralls covered by a sheepskin. To top it off, a flak vest that reached from the neck to the pelvis and was designed to protect from flak splinters and bullets.

We wore sheepskin boots, and tied regular GI shoes on to our belt, in case we had to crash-land in enemy territory. A "Mae West" around the neck; the pilots wore back-pack parachutes and the rest of the crew had chest packs that could clamp on if they had to bail out. You had electrically-heated gloves on your hands that you dared not take off, fearing frostbite. Of course, at high altitude an oxygen mask was worn. Each crew member had a headset and mike connected to the intercom.

Ready For Takeoff*

During the night, armament men arrived at each dispersal area with a load of bombs on their trailers. The target would determine what bombs were to be loaded. They could be 1,000 pounders, 500 pounders, or 100 pounders; and if we were supporting Patton's Third Army or Bradley's

First Army, we might be carrying a load of small anti-personnel bombs that were very dangerous because they could get caught up in the bomb bay. The B24 could carry 8,000 pounds of bombs.

The ground crews followed the armament men. They pushed the propellers by hand to force out any oil that might have collected overnight in the piston cylinders. The crew chief climbed into the cockpit and started the engines. When he was satisfied with their performance, he cut them to save fuel. The crew checked for oil, fuel, and hydraulic leaks, and cleaned the windshield. The bird was ready to fly.

When the rest of the crew arrived, we boarded the plane. We would go over the check list and then start the engines. Then came the waiting, all eyes on the control tower. Finally a green flare lit the sky, the signal to go. The planes would leave their hardstands, get in line and go down the taxi strip to the runway.

Actually, each base had three runways, one 6,000 feet and two about 4,500 feet. Because of the heavy load we usually took off on the 6,000 foot runway. If the weather and wind direction were such that we had to use a shorter runway, we would stand on the brakes and shove the throttles forward. The plane shook. Brakes released, the plane loaded with bombs, ammunition boxes, and more than 2700 gallons of gas roared down the runway and we were airborne. Many planes were lost on takeoff because of the heavy load.

Into Formation*

The plane's position in the formation was given to us at the briefing. There was a diagram on a blackboard with the pilot's name for each position in the formation. Takeoff would be by squadrons. England's winter weather made it difficult to get a formation in the air. Overcast with the base at 400 feet and the top anywhere from 4,000 to 15,000 feet presented a challenge.

Often the takeoff was into a pea-soup fog. A long climb to break out of the clouds was not unusual. Planes might get perilously close to each other. There were times when the control tower could not see the planes rolling down the runway. There were times when you could not see your wing planes, and other times when you couldn't see the tips of your own wings. Lt. Frink was right.

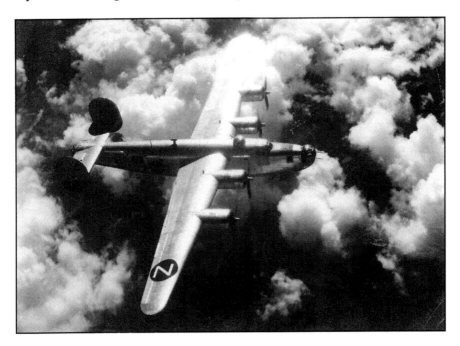

The trick was to get the plane off the ground, climb through the clouds, and come out on top. You had to do this with roughly 36 or 40 planes taking off at 32 second intervals. While climbing through the "soup" on instruments, you might hit the prop-wash from the plane ahead. Prop- wash could get so heavy it could flip a bomber over! You really had to concentrate.

When you were above the cloud cover, you would see planes everywhere—above, below, ahead, behind, and aside. Collisions could occur. The group leader would fire flares of one color. The squadron leaders fired a different color. It took a great deal of time and jockeying before the formation could be on the way to the target.

Years later when I spoke with General Lyle about it, he told me it took about five missions before pilots got pretty good in the forming area. He also told me that once, when they were flying a practice mission, he turned around and flew back through his own formation to show them they weren't flying tight enough.

When you got into formation and on the wing of the plane you were assigned to, you would fly as tight as you could on that one plane and ignore what was going on around you. I learned to "sock it in" about five feet from that plane, and if something happened to him, you found the next plane and would stay with him.

Groups gathered in a slow revolving "racetrack spiral" before forming the bomber train. Once formed, the contrails of a thousand bombers in the sky were a beautiful sight. It will never be seen again. It was 10,000 young men fighting their way to targets in enemy-occupied territory.

Fighter escorts

At our briefing, we found out where and when we would pick up our fighter escorts. Early in the air war over Europe, the first escorts were P38s, the twin-engine Lockheed "Lightning." They had a tough time flying combat against the ME109's and FW 190s. My friends who saw action then said it took the P38s "three time zones to make a turn." They also had another problem: they could stay up only about an hour and a half and couldn't take the bomber train deep into Germany.

The second fighter used for escort was the P47 Thunderbolt. It was a rugged plane, had a high ceiling, and could dive down on the enemy fighters, but its range was also limited. However, with wing tanks it could stay up about two and one half hours.

The fighter that really turned the air war around for us was the P51 Mustang. It arrived in 1943 and could stay up for more than seven and a half hours. It was the best fighter in WW2 and could take the bombers deep into Germany.

To The Target

When our bomber train left the English coast and crossed the channel, the gunners tested their guns. At 10,000 feet we would order the crew to put on their oxygen masks and plug in their heated suits. Seven to eight hours of flying through flak and fighters called for endurance and skill. We found the most effective way was to take turns of 20 minutes and then turn it over to the other guy.

There was a lot of tension involved from the intense concentration. Flying over enemy territory, there was always the possibility of death or spending the rest of the war in a prison camp. Some crashed, others jumped from disabled planes. Hopes were they would fall into the hands of the military. There were times when an airman was captured by civilian mobs and beaten to death or thrown into a burning building. Some never got by their first mission.

On your first mission, the worst feeling was when you realized that people were shooting at you and trying to kill you. We learned by on-the- job training, becoming seasoned veterans as our missions flew by. We developed defensive skills, such as always flying in tight formations. At least flying the plane and monitoring the radio kept you very busy. I felt sorry for the gunners who were waiting for something to happen. The bomber pilot knew what he was to do. He, along with the navigator and nose gunner, had to get the bombs on the target. The gunners had to keep the enemy planes away.

On a typical mission, enemy fighters attacked our airplanes before and after we had bombed our assigned targets, but the gunners in the crew felt they had a chance to defend themselves against those attacks.

At the IP (the initial point), where we would turn to the target and fly a half hour "bomb run", the German 88 anti-aircraft guns would take over and our only defense was "Tinsel." The waist gunners would throw it out to confuse the radar that was tracking us. Flak looks pretty innocent, just puffs of black smoke, but we quickly learned that death and destruction awaited us in those innocent-looking floating clouds. For the half an hour going through it, the tendency was to think, "Can we leave? Can we get out of here now?" We knew we couldn't. Our training taught us to obey commands and follow orders. That is what we had to do and that is what we did. But we also felt that luck became a factor when flying into flak. I felt like "a pebble on a beach"—totally insignificant.

The Ruhr Valley held a great deal of manufacturing, and those cities were heavily armed with anti-aircraft guns. For example, Hamburg, Bremen, and Brunswick had more than 1000 each. The Ruhr was known to us as "Flak Alley." Magdeburg, with its oil refineries, had 900 guns, and Berlin had 2400 anti-aircraft guns. The flak was brutal! To fly through it and not get hit was pure luck.

The Return

As the formation finally approached the target, the lead bombardier took over: "Bomb bay doors open! Bombs away!" I can still see those bombs dropping. At that point, our work for "Uncle Sam" was over but now we had to get back to England.

As we turned back and headed home, the German fighters might return; and as we headed west we could run into some railroad flak batteries that we didn't know about.

After that we might even pick up some tunes on our headsets from "Berlin Sally," like Glenn Miller's "In the Mood," or Benny Goodman's "Don't be that way." Her message might be, "Tomorrow we will destroy the 446th BG." Finally, on our return heading to Bungay and still flying tight formation, we'd peel off into the traffic pattern and land.

At the debriefing we were served a shot of whiskey and some coffee as we discussed the day's mission with the intelligence officer. Sometimes the squadron and group commanders would join in the discussion. Then a shower in our not-too fancy facility, back to the hut for a nap, and then get ready for a little chow and "R&R" that evening.

Reflections

Some days were better than others and some days were those that you could never forget. Even though we wore heated suits to help encounter the extreme cold—45 degrees below zero at high altitudes—I never remember having to turn them on. You were so scared, you'd be perspiring and that kept you warm enough!

Every part of the mission was filled with challenges. Just getting up and into position was some of the most dangerous stuff. Flying planes loaded to the hilt with bombs, fuel, and ammunition for the twelve 50 caliber machine guns was a danger in itself. Crews could be lost to accidents on takeoff or in mid-air collisions, with hundreds of bombers attempting to form up in the cloud-filled skies over England. The enemy fighters, flak over the target and unpredictable weather – each added greatly to the tension. Taken all together, the chances for disaster for your crew were very real each time.

It was very tough. You worked hard. You were scared and you had your neck stuck out; but boy, I wouldn't have missed it for the world! My principal reasons for feeling that way were the life-long friendships I developed with my flying buddies, and the pride which we all shared in our country, like many of us during that era and in subsequent conflicts that have been fought by American servicemen and women with commitment and bravery.

We put it all on the line because we knew The Price of Freedom!

---

* An article was produced by my 446th Bomb Group Association from Air Force periodicals, diaries, and group newsletters. This section is adapted from that article.

CHAPTER 14
April 1945

I have just described the general mission experience, but a bombing mission over enemy territory was never routine. There was imminent danger lurking from takeoff to landing. You had to be physically and mentally prepared for any unsuspected crisis. An engine could be lost on takeoff or anywhere during the flight. When reaching the forming area, one of the planes in your squadron or group could slide into you or you into them. Weather was unpredictable and you had no control over enemy action from fighters or anti-aircraft guns.

File photo of my B24 on mission

I had many close calls but there were two missions that stand out in my mind as times that God winked at me – on back-to-back days in April of 1945.

The first day was a small but violent mission in which our Group Commander, Colonel Crawford, went missing in action, and we lost 2 of our 23 planes. We had to divert to our secondary target, Wesendorf Airfield, after the primary was cloud covered.

Colonel Crawford was flying in a British Mosquito to observe the mission. Before the formation reached the target, one FW190 in the lead and eight to fifteen ME262s – the first jet fighters in the war—attacked us from the front; then circled to make attacks from six to seven o'clock. We were flying at about 20,000 feet when the jets were attacking. Colonel Crawford called the formation leader from his Mosquito and said he was joining the formation for the protection of our machine guns. During this attack, while monitoring the radio, I heard someone yell, "Somebody hit the Colonel!" I was sure friendly fire had brought him down – some protection!

ME 262 – First Jet Fighter

We were flying low left in the formation, and right after that, our left waist gunner, "Pappy" French, shouted that an ME 262 was right on top of us. All the guns on our left side were firing, including the top turret. The shell casings were dropping into the cockpit from the gun. I heard Jack Tardieu, our flight engineer, yell from his gun position, "We got him!" The kill was later verified and we got credit for shooting down the German jet.

Despite the fighter attacks, our group hit Wesendorf which was an ME262 airfield and strike photos showed bursts on the eastern third of the airfield including the runway. However, several of the 446 BG planes were hit that day.

Colonel Crawford was listed as missing action. On April 16, the group received word he was safe after release from a POW camp by ground forces. He returned to the group April 22, still complaining about our marksmanship.

Lt. Dick Lawson's "Shoo Shoo Baby" was hit—we had seen the black smoke go up from the crash and we thought they were goners. After debriefing, we were watching for them because we knew they were in serious trouble. The pilot and copilot lived in our barracks. They came into the mess hall that night still wearing their parachute harnesses, shouting, "We hope you guys didn't take any of our gear in the barracks!" They had made it back to within seven miles of our air base where the crew bailed out safely. The plane had to be abandoned because the hydraulic system was out—the left landing gear could not be extended, and the engines were cutting out.

It was great to see them alive and kicking!

We later learned that Lt. Bob Free of the 706th squadron and his crew landed on the Continent after leaving the formation with their number three engine feathered and the number four engine smoking.

It was an exciting day for us but I soon found out we would be on our way again tomorrow. This time, it was weather that would give us a narrow escape from death—not only me and my crew but hundreds of other crews as well.

We went to an early morning briefing in some lousy weather. We learned that our target for the day was the ball bearing factory in Bayreuth, Germany. It would be a very long mission, a "three candy bar affair." The weather was so bad that we were ordered to form near Paris where there would be a break in the clouds at about 10,000 feet, and we would meet B24s from the Second Air Division.

When we left the briefing room, it was still pouring rain. I went for communion with Father Murphy, and then went to my "locker" (This wasn't like the lockers at Yankee Stadium). At best, they were very shabby.

My friend Ed Beebe had a locker next to mine, and we were discussing what we might expect on that day's mission. Reverend Gannon, the Protestant Chaplain, stopped by to wish us luck. He gave us a laugh when he said he went on a mission a few weeks before and was in the "waist" with the gunners. When they started throwing the "tinsel" out, he helped but left the wrappers on so that he might do as much damage as possible.

I wished Ed good luck and we agreed to meet that night when we returned to the base.

I taxied into position for take-off at the end of a short runway but you couldn't even see the end of it. The tower cleared us for take-off and away we went. We reached our assigned altitude and headed for Paris in "instruments only" weather. As we crossed the Channel, red tracers started flying across our nose. Evidently some gunners were testing their guns—not a good idea when there were hundreds of planes heading for the remote forming area in horrible weather and on instruments!

When we reached the forming area and found a break in the clouds, we could see about two hundred B24s circling in an oval "race track" formation. We soon realized there was no chance of finding our Group or our Squadron. We were in a torrential rain storm, thunder and lightning was all around us—the rain was even coming through the windshield. There was only one thing to do—we had to abort the mission and try to get home.

But we had no visibility and our only navigational aid was our compass. We had to let down; fly low below the clouds; and head west to find the English Channel. We spotted several more B24s with different group markings having the same problem.

After flying in those conditions for about thirty minutes under dead reckoning, we found ourselves all alone over water--still fighting heavy rain, wind, and poor visibility; but what was this body of water? It was too small to be the Channel – it had to be the Bay of Antwerp and we must have been pushed way north by the strong winds. Obviously we had missed the barrage balloons that filled and surrounded the Bay. Now we knew where we were, and going west would take us to the channel.

But what about those barrage balloons we knew were thick in this area? We decided to leave the water as soon as we could, heading west. As we left the water, we were almost brushing the leaves on the trees but then could pull up a little; find the friendly English Channel, and head for our air base at Bungay.

Pin-up Girl's crew (Ed Beebe at lower left)

We had been totally lost, but landed late in the afternoon as other planes were straggling in from the aborted mission to Bayreuth. The weather had really hurt us that day, and we waited to see if everyone got back safely. I continued to hang around the control tower to see if my friend Ed Beebe in "Pin-up Girl" had made it. There was no word and the plane was declared "Missing in Action." "Damn, there go some more good guys!" Well, maybe they crash-landed and were in the underground somewhere, or at worst, taken prisoner. We hoped to get some good news, but the weather that day was so bad, anything could have happened to them.

* * * * * * * * * * * * *

In May of 1945, I was still waiting for orders to take off for our trip back to the states and I received a pencil-written note from Ed Beebe. He had written it from a hospital bed in Belgium while recuperating from the injuries he had received while trying to save his crew.

They had gone through the same foul weather that we had; but they were not so lucky. The wind had taken them over German-occupied territory in Holland and they were hit with small arms fire and anything else the Germans could get their hands on.

A fire broke out in the bomb bay, so Ed grabbed a fire extinguisher and went back to see if he could help his flight engineer and two other crew members put it out. He quickly decided it was hopeless and told them to bail out. Then he returned to the cockpit to help the pilot and found he wasn't there—he had "taken a powder."

Ed, suffering from a flak wound in his right leg and burned hands and face, got into his seat and tried to talk to the rest of the crew on the intercom—but it had been burned out. He decided to release the bombs so that he could attempt a landing, but his hands were so badly burned he couldn't pull the handle. To make matters worse, the wheels had fallen down. He figured that were still a few guys on board so he would try the impossible – - land a burning B24 with a bomb load and wheels down in a field that was probably muddy.

After the crash landing, there were still three alive—the tail gunner, the navigator and Ed. The Germans who captured them wouldn't tell them about anyone else. The tail gunner had a few broken

144

ribs; the navigator had a badly sprained ankle and found out later that he had a broken bone in his back. Ed had a broken left leg, a flak-hole in his right leg, burned face and hands and a paralyzed right arm. The Germans imprisoned them but they were soon freed by Canadian ground forces and taken to an American hospital.

As soon as I received the letter, I showed it to all our friends who were happy to know that he was in safe hands again. My immediate reaction was that he had performed heroically and deserved a medal for saving the remaining members of his crew, while ignoring the major wounds he had received.

I went to headquarters and tried to find the Special Services Officer, but he had already left for the States with most of the cadre. There was no one there who could help me get anything accomplished. There was no alternative but to trust that men in his crew would take care of the situation.

Forty-seven years later I found Ed's address in the Mighty Eighth's Museum library in Savannah, GA and I contacted him. He told me that he was a bartender in Connecticut. I tried to get him to come down and visit the museum, but he said that he couldn't go anywhere. Two months later, I received a phone call from Ed Beebe, Jr. He said his dad had passed away and when going through his things, he found a letter that I had sent him. Then he said, "What kind of a man was my father? We weren't very close." I said, "Your dad was a super star, an American hero, he should have been awarded the Congressional Medal of Honor! You should be very proud of him!" Ed's son said to me, "Thank you, I didn't know that."

CHAPTER 15

Out of Europe

Leaving Europe

On April 25, 1945, the air war in Europe ended.

I spent a few days flying ground personnel from our base and other fighter bases over Germany so they could see the damage done during the air war. We called it "A Tour of The Ruhr." That was the official word, but down deep inside I really believed the main purpose was to let the Germans know we had tremendous air power. When we flew over the autobahns, as far as you could see there were six lanes of our tanks, armored trucks, artillery equipment, and all other types of military equipment. In other words, "Remain calm; there is no sense in fighting any longer."

On May 6th, I went to London for a three-day leave, and on May 8th the Germans officially surrendered. For the first time since 1939, the lights went on in this great city. The British people had real reason to celebrate and it was exciting to be there with them. However, many of the Americans in the city that night had Japan on their mind. I realized that my next assignment would be B29 training and the South Pacific. We were very happy but realistic; and even though General Eisenhower gave everyone an extra day of leave, I headed back to the base to find out what was going on.

We received our orders: Early in June, we would fly our B24 back to the States via Prestwick, Scotland; Iceland; Goose Bay, Labrador; Presque Isle, Maine; and Bradley Field, Conn. We would carry 20 ground personnel with us and we were to get thirty-day leaves.

The B24 wasn't built for comfort. It would make the trip of 25 hours a very tough ride for a bunch of homesick soldiers. However, this was our number one priority. We had to get these guys home safely and we did it without a hitch.

When we touched down at Presque Isle, Maine, our valuable cargo yelled and shouted. They were back in the wonderful U.S. of A. There to greet us were a half dozen beautiful Red Cross girls, wearing real silk stockings. They showed us the way to the mess hall for a great lunch while the plane was being checked out and refueled.

We had one more leg to fly and that was to Bradley Field. Our baggage went through a complete inspection and we turned in all our combat gear. Then we left for Westover Field, where we received orders for reassignment (after our thirty day leave) to Sioux Falls, South Dakota, and to wait there for a B29 training destination.

Sioux Falls And Out

Sioux Falls was absolutely mobbed with airmen returning from the U.K., France, Italy, and North Africa. The Army Air Corps hadn't prepared very well for this many men. To get the base under control they brought in "Killer" Kane, of Ploesti air raid fame, now a General. He lasted about a week.

The first day he restricted everyone to the base, so we spent the day in line at the mess hall. The second and third day, a few other guys and I found out that local farmers needed help with their crops and promised a decent meal. So we volunteered.

Six of us, including two Colonels, shucked 55 acres of oats the first day, and 35 acres the second day, and had fine meals at the farm house.

Heading back to the base, we stopped in a tiny saloon at a remote crossroad while waiting for a truck to pick us up. While we downed a refreshing cold beer, the owner turned on a radio behind the bar. It blared out that the Atomic Bomb had been dropped on Hiroshima and Nagasaki, and that the Japanese were surrendering. Talk about excitement! The War was over!

That night Sioux Falls hosted the biggest and wildest party I have ever been to or would ever go to for the rest of my life. Then all we had to wait for were our orders. When I received mine I found that before being discharged, I had to go again to Harlingen, Texas.

The air base at Sioux Falls had a huge marshaling yard, and I remember spending at least six hours with thousands of guys waiting to get called to board a train. Finally, we were called. The train cars had to be from the civil war. They were wooden with old fashioned seats; and to top it off, when darkness fell, one of the train hands came through and lit a gas lamp on each end of the car.

We were grimy when we reached Houston. We got a chance to get off and go to a YMCA to get cleaned up, grab a bite to eat, and then get back to the station. Our car had been hooked on to the last car of another train heading for Harlingen.

The second day while we were working out our orders for discharge, we were allowed to fly our required four hours for each month that we hadn't flown. It was worth 75 dollars per month, and I would make 150 dollars by flying a B24 four hours in the morning and four hours in the afternoon.

My morning flight was fine. When I went back to the operations room in the afternoon, the dispatcher arranged for me to have another plane. He said it would be ready in about a half hour. After about ten minutes, he called me over and told me there were two first pilots that had gone to England, but were too late to fly any missions. Would I mind flying with them since I had already flown in the morning? I said "no problem."

I got in the right seat and one of the guys got in the left seat. He kind of fumbled around so I told him to start the engines. He had trouble starting them, so I began to get a little suspicious. I called the tower and we got permission to taxi to the runway. I noticed that this guy wasn't too good at it. Now, I was skeptical. I called the tower and they cleared us to go.

We started down the runway. We needed 125 miles per hour to get the B24 airborne. This guy had his feet partially on the brake pedals and we were moving too slowly. I yelled at the flight engineer to get him out of the way, so he flipped the lever behind the seat and the guy flew about three feet back from the controls.

I waited until the last seconds and eased off the runway, brushing the tree tops at the end of the field. I knew the flight engineer; he had been in my squadron at the 446 BG. I asked him "What's with those two stiffs?" He told me that he had overheard them talking on the flight deck and they only had a few hours in a B24; they had never been overseas, and they wanted to see if they could fly from the left seat.

I was livid. I flew around for four hours, landed and got out of the plane. Since I was getting out of the service, I told them exactly what I thought of them and left them standing on the tarmac. After all I had been through, it would have been a sad ending to wind up in a ball of flames at the end of a 75 dollar flight.

The mission was complete; soon I would be a civilian!

Next Steps

Another very critical time of my life was October, 1945. WWII had ended and it was necessary for me to get on with my life. The first morning when I woke up after almost four years in the military, it was a very lonesome feeling. There were no orders to go to "link training" or to be at the flight line at a specific time. We were now on our own again and the decisions that I made, good or bad, would lay out my life plan for me.

The United States Government had passed a law called the GI Bill of Rights. This was the greatest thing that could have happened for me and more than 2,000,000 other veterans of WWII. Most of us never could have afforded to go to college, but the GI Bill gave us the opportunity to get our degrees.

It turned out to be not only for our own benefit but, most importantly, for the United States of America. It would prove to be the engine that took our country from an all-out war effort to the powerful nation we are today. It made engineers, accountants, doctors, lawyers, and business professionals out of soldiers, sailors, marines, coastguardsmen and airmen.

Fortunately, I had the sense to take advantage of that opportunity and that step led me down a rewarding path. I am now dedicated to helping guide our nation's current youth to rewards of their own.

CHAPTER 16

On to College

I had always wanted to go to Notre Dame and their next semester would begin in March of 1946. I sent away for the application, and after completing it and sending it in, I was accepted and could begin in the spring semester. While still in uniform, I decided to visit Lafayette College where I had served in the Air Cadet College Training program. During that program, the commandant had organized a fast pitch softball team. We had a great team and we went around and played colleges in the eastern Pennsylvania area.

When I walked into the Athletic Director's office, he was pleased to see me and said, "I want you to meet our new baseball coach, Charlie Gelbert." The first thing I noted on Charlie's desk was a picture of him in his Naval Officer's uniform and another in his St. Louis Cardinal's uniform. He was my kind of guy.*

We talked about the war, baseball, and education. I told him I was going to go to Notre Dame in the spring and he said, "Why don't you go up to the admissions office and see if you can get accepted here? Then you can be my catcher in March. We have a lot of good players coming back from the service and you can join them." I hadn't played in four years, but I knew that Lafayette had had some great baseball

---

Gelbert was the Cardinals' starting shortstop from 1929-32, including the pennant winning team of 1930 as well as the team that won the 1931 World Series. He finished 25th in voting for the 1931 National League MVP. He played in 131 games and had 447 at bats, 61 runs, 129 hits, and a .289 batting average.

Charlie's career nearly ended when he severely injured his left ankle in a hunting accident. He won the "Most Courageous Athlete Award" in 1935 when he came back after being out for two years. He spent the rest of his baseball career as a utility infielder for the Cincinnati Reds, Detroit Tigers, Washington Senators, and the Boston Red Sox. Source:Wikipedia

teams before the war. With this guy coaching, they were going to have some great teams again

Charlie called admissions and I was accepted. I decided to start at Lafayette in the February semester. Charlie Gelbert was a terrific man and he helped me and many others get back into civilian life and become good citizens and successful college students.

* * * * * * * * * * * * *

Returning to my father for a moment, I recall vividly my trip to start my years at Lafayette. The college was about 80 miles from where we lived and it took about two hours to drive there. He and I drove up to school in the same old 1939 Chevrolet and Pop never said one word to me the whole way. When I took my things out of the car at Gates Hall, he said, "Your sister-in-law said last night that you would never make it." Is that motivation or what!

She got the first invitation to my graduation in June of 1948. The only thing that mattered to my father was for me to graduate from college. He knew the value of a college education. He knew that without it you would regret it the rest of your life!

* * * * * * * * * * * * *

When I went into the Army Air Corps, I met people who had college degrees and those that had not had that opportunity. You could tell the difference in their confidence level and their communication skills.

A college degree is a very important step for anyone that wishes to be a success in life. It not only increases your knowledge from the courses that you are taking but it teaches you responsibility, leadership, and the ability to get along with people . It gives you a sense of accomplishment in the competitive world that we live in and opens doors to fields that you may wish to pursue. Further, it introduces you to career paths you may never have considered—in business, engineering, science or the arts. Perhaps most importantly, you learn that to succeed in whatever path you choose, you must have goals and apply yourself to them.

Our nation was the winner in the GI Bill program as we broke away from an all out war effort to putting our greatest generation back to work.

* * * * * * * * * * * * * *

My first day at college was a busy one. I went to the Dean's office and got credit for my two semesters of night school with the Van Tassel twins at Bergen Jr. College in 1941, for my semester and a half at V.P.I., and a couple more from the military. As a result, if I attended two summer schools in addition to regular classes, I could obtain my degree in June of 1948 at the age of 25.

* * * * * * * * * * * * * *

Charlie treated us veterans like men. It took someone like him to keep us in line. I had great respect for him because he had been in the service. After being a star shortstop with the famous "Gas House Gang" and shooting himself in a hunting accident, he fought back and made the most of a tough break.

We became great friends while I attended Lafayette and we continued our friendship after college. We had just returned from war and even though we were only a couple months removed from combat, we had to become college students. Charlie led us through the transition. He could really lay the law down and, on top of that, he was a very caring family man. We became a part of his family. When I became the alumni representative on the Board of Trustees at Lafayette, he was always there for consultation.

Charlie served as coach of the Lafayette baseball team for 21 years and the team I was on in 1948 went to the first NCAA College World Series double-elimination format. We had to beat about 10 Division 1 universities to get to the semi-finals where we lost to Yale, who went on to lose to Southern California. Incidentally, President Bush played first base for Yale.

I'll always remember one Friday night in 1967 when we lived on Long Island and I was driving home from work. The news came over the radio that Charlie had died while walking home from his office at

Lafayette. I pulled the car off the road and cried. He was my Hall of Fame MVP and a man of great character.

CHAPTER 17

Character
In Business

In our lifetimes we meet many people. Most create memories – some fleeting, some unforgettable. During my working career of nearly seventy years, there were several people who deeply touched me and whose character traits are worth sharing. You will meet Elmer Shaver, Walt Nielsen, Bob Chepak, and Bob Carr. Their examples honed my skills, shaped my character and enriched my life.

My plan to graduate from Lafayette in June of 1948 was working. I had attended summer school in 1946 and 1947, and using the credits I had earned before entering the military and during my service in WWII, I had enough to get my degree.

Toward the end of my senior year, I began taking job interviews with a number of companies visiting our campus. The "GI Bill" was working beautifully, and most of us who were graduating that year were veterans of WWII. A career was the most important thing we had to establish. I was married and had a wife and son to support.

Charley Gelbert told me I should get into baseball because I would make an excellent manager. However, I thought my best answer would be a job with a large corporation in the purchasing department, advertising, or some other area where I could take home a steady paycheck. There was another thing—we had to find a place to live.

Starting My Working Career

One of the interviews was with The Burroughs Adding Machine Co. Two of their representatives, Don Fritts and Bill Gifford, came to the campus and tried to convince me that I should go to work as a marketing representative or, in simpler terms, a salesman. They invited me to New York City to take a test and see their offices at Eighteenth Street and Park Avenue South. I agreed, and since we were playing N.Y.U. in a couple weeks, I could combine the trip with a visit to Burroughs. Everything went well and I was hired. I'd start the week after I graduated from Lafayette. Incidentally, I caught the game at Ohio Field in Upper Manhattan and had three hits. The win put us in line for a trip to the College World Series.

This put a bit of a crimp in my business career because it would delay my start at Burroughs for a couple weeks. Wade Duym, a Phi Delta Theta fraternity brother and one of my best friends, arranged for me to live with his parents in Cliffside Park, NJ, until Jeanne and I could find housing within commuting distance of New York City. Wade still had another year of college. He was a star basketball player who had transferred from St. Johns to Lafayette.

We lost to Yale in the semifinals; it was time for me to forget fun and games and get to work. I arrived at Burroughs June 15, 1948. About ten other recruits had begun two weeks earlier. Let me describe what the Burroughs sales office was like in those days in New York City.

There were about one hundred and twenty men milling around—some wearing fedoras, some homburgs, the rest bare-headed. They were smoking cigarettes, cigars, and pipes, while reading the Daily News, The Mirror, The Herald Tribune, The New York Times, or the Daily Telegraph Racing News. While this was going on, one of the ten Zone Managers would call the roll and each salesman (please note there were no lady sales people—they were trainers and installers) would report yesterday's sales.

Our product line at that time was adding machines, cash machines, calculators, and bookkeeping machines (The "Moon- Hopkins," a large machine that had a combination keyboard and/or a mechanical multiplying section), and large bank posting machines. There were no electronics.

Burroughs had 135 direct sales branches. New York City and the sub-office in Newark, NJ were the only dealerships in the company.

The owner of the dealerships was A.E. Spaldorf, a man about seventy years of age who sat in the corner office. My first morning, he walked out of his office and said to me, "You're a little late sliding into second base, aren't you young man?" I said, "Yes sir, who are you?" He answered, "I own the place. What will your goal be while you are working here?" I said, "I'd like your job." Little did I know that 23 years later, I would have it.

After going through sales training on all the equipment, I was transferred to the sub-office in Newark. In January of 1949, the name "Burroughs Adding Machine Co." was changed to "Burroughs Corporation." A.E. Spaldorf retired and New York City and Newark became direct branches. We had a new Branch Manager from Buffalo, New York, Elmer Shaver.

Shaver wore a homburg and a Chesterfield overcoat. The day he arrived, he walked into his office, hung them up, walked into the sales office, and sat down with all the salesmen. This guy was in command. He knew what everyone's sales were and what their quota was. He was finding out what was being sold, and finding out all he could about each salesman.

The last day of the month, he called us all in at 8:00 AM. He knew what each person had sold during the month. He said, "We need 5,000 dollars of sales to reach one hundred percent of quota." We never knew what "quota" was before that. He said, "Who can get an order today?" I raised my hand. He said, "How much?" I said, "5,000 dollars." He then asked me, "Why haven't you closed the sale?" I told him I had been trying for four months. It's an automobile dealer and he refuses to sign." Elmer walked into his office, put his hat and coat on and said, "Let's go."

It took 35 minutes to drive to the dealership and he never asked me about the deal. He loved the fact that his name was Elmer, "because the customers can never forget that name." He said his best friends were his customers and his prospects.

He told me that when he shaved in the morning, he did it in front of a sun lamp so he could be tan in the winter like his successful customers who went to Florida on vacation. He would take bankers and CEOs to Canada on fishing trips. He said, "They're the ones who can sign orders." He knew he was the best salesman in any branch he managed, and his branches had made quota every month for the last five years.

At the Ford dealer's office, I introduced Elmer. Mr. Myers, the dealer, said to him, "What's the reason for your visit?" Elmer said, "Paul tells me he's having a problem with you." Myers said, "We aren't having a problem!" Elmer said, "Well he's having a problem with me. What's keeping you from signing the order?" Myers said, "We want to try it for thirty days." Elmer said "Paul, give him that contract". I said, "Uh which contract?" Elmer said, "Just write on it 'We will pay after machine is installed for thirty days.'" Mr. Myers signed and we're out of there.

On the way back in the car, Elmer said, "When you get the order, get out!" Then he asked me, "How much are you going to sell this year?" I replied with enthusiasm, "Sixty thousand dollars!" He said, "When we get back to the branch, turn in your resignation." I said, "One hundred thousand!" He said, "Forget the resignation, now you're a salesman!"

What an education I had the last day of January in 1949—not only about selling but about managing salesmen as well. I became the top salesman in the branch and Elmer Shaver was appointed manager of the Detroit Branch. This was the crown jewel of Burroughs' branches, because it was the location of the home office.

Just before he left Newark, Elmer took me with him to a department store as he bought his new wardrobe for his next conquest. As we walked back to the branch, Elmer asked, "You're me and what is the first thing you're going to do?" I said, "Get up in front of those sixty hot shots and tell them you've made your quota every month for the last seven years and you're expected to do the same thing here! If you're wondering, who's the best salesman in the room; forget it. I am." Elmer said, "You've got it. You're on your way."

Onwards And Upwards

In the summer of 1951, my new Branch manager in Newark told me I was to go to Detroit and see the general sales manager about a job in the home office. It was to run the exhibit center, where I would demonstrate all the latest equipment to customers and marketing people from all over the United States and around the world. The general sales manager had asked Elmer if I was a good demonstrator. Elmer told him not to worry—if that was part of the job requirement, I could handle it easily. That was my first move.

After that, I became the sales promotion manager for adding machines, cash registers, and calculators for the United States and Canada. I visited every one of the U.S. branches and most of the Canadian branches.

Then followed: zone sales manager in New York City; branch manager in Wilmington, Delaware; branch manager in Hempstead, Long Island; and district manager in Syracuse, NY. After five months in Syracuse, I was asked to take over the district in New York City that covered Manhattan, northern NJ, Long Island, Brooklyn and Westchester. There were 500 employees in the District. The sales quota reached 45 million dollars.

Many people helped me get to this point in this great adventure. I recently was reading about the Beech Aircraft Company and its matriarch, Olive Ann Beech. She never had a college education but was always surrounded with inspirational sayings and had built an extremely successful company. She quoted Norman Vincent Peale and "His Power of Positive Thinking" which is quite apropos:

"You can't expect your ships to come home unless you send them out.

Stand up to be seen. Speak up to be heard. Shut up to be appreciated.

No one can make you feel inferior without your consent."

New York is a tough market, and any success you might have in that environment is a very fulfilling accomplishment. After having been there for a year and a half, I realized I had no problem from a marketing standpoint, but I really needed help in the financial and accounting area to meet the required profit margins.

The home office sent a young man from Minneapolis named Walt Nielsen. He had been well trained and knew how a financial control manager should operate a district.

We became very close and it worked like a charm. He took care of the financial side and I took care of the marketing side. He had all 16 of our branches operating within the rules, reporting properly, and setting their sights at profit margins. You cannot hide good people, and after four years, he was called back to the home office to manage distribution operations for the company.

I really missed Walt and his operational expertise. After a couple years, management sent a new, highly qualified young man with a great deal of large-systems experience and a bright future with the company to replace me. I told my staff and management people that Bob Chepak would be their new manager, and that he was well qualified to help them and their families become very successful. I was going to New Jersey and would be operating a banking branch.

Transitions

My ego took quite a hit. Sons Terry and Bob were married and on their own, but we still had Marianne starting high school and Gary starting at Notre Dame. There was no way I could think about retiring at 58.

Late one afternoon, months later, Bob Chepak walked into my office in New Jersey and said, "Hi Paul, let's go across the street and have a drink." I hadn't spoken to or seen him since he had taken over the New York District. I said, "That will be great, let's go."

We sat there for an hour and had a very fine discussion. He was kind enough to let management know what he had discovered about me: That I thought of the company first, my people and my family next and myself last. That made me feel very good because it's what I always tried to do.

Within a year, Bob Chepak would become the New York Financial Manger and my boss. We became very close friends.

Bob Chepak

I had become more and more involved with direct selling; in fact, ADP bank services had become a very important direct account. We began getting their check processing service centers and savings bank services business.

In the mean time, Bob had New York Financial operating successfully. He could make the most effective calls on high level management that I had ever seen. He immediately gained their respect and those are the guys who can sign orders!

Soon I had another career decision. Burroughs had merged with Univac and we became the Unisys Corporation. I became eligible to take early retirement. Bob and I talked about it and it sounded like a pretty good deal. I would be paid one half of my prior-year earnings for four years, when I would become sixty- three. I was confident that I could be able to continue to earn enough to maintain our way of life.

I was offered a position at ADP as Assistant to the vice president of marketing, but I decided that I would like to have my own company. Working with Data Systems of NJ gave me that opportunity, and I began selling computer systems to country clubs.

Bob Chepak left Unisys to become President of Sweda International. He purchased a computer from me for his country club. While we were installing it he said, as only he could say, "Why don't you stop this nonsense and become my director of large account marketing?" He had a little trouble getting a guy 63 hired, but he pulled it off and I was back in the cash register business.

We travelled around the country together and became like family. We did a lot of work, had a lot of fun, and played some golf. He even sent me out to lay the ground work to buy a NAPA Auto Parts servicing operation.

Bob did a great job with the company. Then along came a small group of Swedes and Brits, who bought this division of Litton Industries and tried to run it themselves. They were not competent and they wouldn't listen to Bob's advice, so he had no alternative but to leave. He went on to greater success. He became president of Merrill International and lived in London with his wife Barbara (a super hostess) for ten years. Their lovely daughter Michelle lost a battle with cancer, but her legacy will live on through her niece Ella and her nephew Jack.

Bob Chepak and I have been friends for more than 30 years. I admire people who can put aside their own ambitions long enough to give someone else a hand when it's needed. It's called "Trustworthiness" in the pillars of Character.

Walt Nielsen was transferred to Atlanta by Burroughs to help a new district manager get started. When his job was finished, he left the company and started his own window business—marketing skylights and solarium windows. He became a multi-millionaire; over-extended the business, and lost his fortune. He then came back to rebuild his business; recover all his losses, and make it even stronger. He's now retired. Successful people never give up. This is called "Responsibility."

Working Retirement

Nancy and I moved to Savannah in 1988 to enjoy our life style and my "retirement," However, I needed to have some sort of employment. While working with Sweda, I heard about credit card processing. I called on CitiCorp in New York to put together a national program for their reps to sell cash registers—one that wouldn't interfere with our direct sales force or our dealers.

We had sales training sessions in Los Angeles, San Francisco, Dallas, and New York. I had met the people in charge of the operation, so I contacted them and became a rep in the Savannah and Hilton Head area – or wherever I might be able to get an order. But I found that working for a New York bank in the south was like "selling buggy whips in Detroit."

I had another line to sell, "Check Guarantee," which wasn't very lucrative to say the least. One day I went into Colonial Oil to pick up an order for three of their gas stations. While I was in their office, someone from the purchasing department told me a young man wanted to talk to me. He was installing an inventory system at their gas pumps.

He was Bob Carr. I told him that I represented CitiCorp, he said, "Why don't you work with us? We have six people and you can be the manager down here. The name of my company is Credit Card Software Systems." (I wish I had taken him up on the management suggestion.) I told Bob I was "kind of retired" and only wanted to work two days a week. He said, "Ok, you've got it," and he gave me his card.

The next time he was in Savannah, we made a couple of calls and I said to myself, "This guy is terrific." His partner, Don Lassiter got in touch and we were off and running.

But working as an independent sales operative in credit card sales is a true test of your sales ability. It puts a third party into your game plan who has to be paid too. However, I love entrepreneurs and Bob Carr has to be one of the greatest that ever lived. His track record has proved it. During those early days as he added salesmen to the company, he had to borrow money a few times to pay us, but he always came through!

Bob was at a wedding in St. Louis around 1995 where he met the chairman of the Heartland Bank. Heartland at that time was worth about $900,000,000. The chairman told Bob that he wanted to get into the credit card business. He couldn't have asked a better person, because when he asked Bob if he would run it, it was a done deal.

Of course, it's history now. Bob, his finance man Allan Atkins, and Don Lassiter, bought the company back from Heartland. They were the risk takers. Now the company has a flourishing payroll processing business to go with its credit card processing. It has 3,000 employees and is listed on the New York Stock Exchange. It's also built on the six pillars of "Character Counts."

Bob Carr has always proven to me that character counts. He has never asked for, nor needed, an explanation for any situation or problem that has come up. He is a very trusting person—the kind of person who would never lie to you nor cheat you, and he expects you to act in the same manner.

When we were a small company, CCSS, you could see it in action. In the 25 years I have worked with him, he has never let me down. I give him a lot of the credit for my reaching 90 years of age. When an issue was corrected, his hand was behind the scene, anywhere in the company with no fanfare. I have heard him say, "We have never cheated a customer." I have used that with customers because I know that to be a fact.

Responsibility is another of his character traits: Be accountable, pursue excellence, exercise self control, be proactive-plan and set goals, be persistent, chose positive attitudes, be reflective, set a good example, do your duty, be self reliant.

How about caring? That is—to show love, regard, or concern for the well-being of others. "Never believe that a few caring people can't change the world. For indeed that is all that ever have." Margaret Meade. Bob Carr –"Give Something Back Foundation!"

If any young people reading these words wish someday to be a captain of industry, please take heed of this great poem.

If

Rudyard Kipling

"If you can keep your head when all about you

Are losing theirs and blaming it on you;

If you can trust yourself when all men doubt you;

But make allowance for their doubting too;

If you can wait and not get tired of waiting,

Or, being lied about, don't deal in lies,

Or, being hated, don't give way to hating,

And yet don't look to good, nor talk to wise;

If you can dream – and not make dreams your master;

If you can think—and not make thoughts your aim;

If you can meet with triumph and disaster

And treat those two imposters just the same;

If you can bear to hear the truth you've spoken

Twisted by knaves to make a trap for fools

Or watch the things you gave your life to be broken,

And stop and build 'em up with worn out tools;

If you can make one heap of all your winnings

And risk it on one turn of pitch-an-toss,

And lose, and start again at your beginnings

And never breathe a word about your loss;

If you can force your heart and nerve and sinew

To serve your turn after they are gone,

And so hold on when there is nothing in you

Except the will that says to them: "Hold on";

If you can talk with crowds and keep your virtue,

Or walk with kings- nor lose the common touch;

If neither foes nor loving friends can hurt you;

If all men count with you, but none too much;

If you can fill the unforgiving minute

With sixty seconds' worth of distance run –

Yours is the earth and everything that's in it,

And—which is more – You'll be a man my son"

CHAPTER 18

Mighty Eighth Museum and Character Counts!

The Mighty Eighth Air Force Museum

Nancy and I moved into our new Savannah home in March of 1989. We were here only a few months when I received a call from Joe Jones inviting us to attend a meeting of The Mighty Eighth Air Force Historical Society at Hunter Air Base. We had a very interesting evening, joined the organization, and began attending meetings regularly.

It is worth noting that Joe was quite a guy and had been written up in Ripley's "Believe It Or Not." He was tail gunner on a B17. While his plane was getting into formation, it collided with another B17 in the forming area. Everyone on both the planes was killed except Joe, who was trapped in the tail gunner position at 12,000 feet. All he could do was sit there while the tail section came down and settled in some trees. He was knocked out and suffered a bad tongue bite. The underground picked him up and got him back to his group in England.

It wasn't too long before I became the Wing Commander. We were part of the Georgia Chapter, out of Atlanta, and we were also watching the development of the Heritage Center Museum in Pooler, Georgia.

By the time the Museum opened on May 15, 1996, I had been Wing Commander three times, and was serving my fourth term as board chairman, and now would be serving as a volunteer at the Museum. I'm beginning my 18th year as a volunteer and am now a trustee on the Board.

One of the World's Most Powerful Museum Experiences

We have just changed the name of the museum to The National Museum of The Mighty Eighth Air Force. The Eighth Air Force was activated in Savannah 71 years ago in 1942. It was the largest air armada ever assembled, and took to the skies to defeat the most powerful air force in the world, the German Luftwaffe. The Eighth is still alive and well today. The planning for the Museum was begun by Major General Lewis Lyle, a bomb group commander, over thirty years ago. Today it carries out a mission to preserve for all Americans the stories of courage, character, and patriotism displayed by the men and women of the Eighth Air Force from World War II to the present.

One of General Lyle's objectives when planning the Museum was to "get these stories out to young people. They need to know about character and the price of freedom." Today the Museum is proud to impact the lives of thousands of children through education programs focusing on World War II history and character education.

Character Counts!

Classrooms and schools have changed quite a bit since WWII. While technology has made huge strides for the better, the behavior and character of students have declined markedly. Everyone has seen the statistics and news stories about the difficulties schools nationwide are experiencing with unruly classrooms. Students lack the basic tools to be successful.

The Museum—with thousands of stories that demonstrate strong, admirable character traits—realized it had a unique opportunity to educate students in both history and character. After much research, the Museum decided that the "Character Counts! Program," developed by the Josepheson Institute of Ethics, would be a great approach to this task.

Character Counts! is a non-denominational, nation-wide program with documented success. It emphasizes the importance of the six universally accepted traits critical to good character: Trustworthiness, Respect, Responsibility, Fairness, Caring, and Citizenship.

The Museum and the Chatham County School District began a partnership to help schools implement "Character Counts!" The Museum has funded this partnership to help impact every student's life in a positive, meaningful way.

The great thing about "Character Counts!" is that it intertwines seamlessly into the curriculum teachers and staff already use. It does not require additional class time or create more work for overburdened teachers. The academics of literature, science, social studies, history, and even math are integrated with six traits. Teachers can use their everyday lessons to encourage students to think critically about character, and how good decision-making can be applied. This creates a common language for the students by consistently emphasizing and using examples of the six pillars. The Museum began training teachers and staff in August 2010, and continued throughout the year until every school in the district had been trained in the program. The all-day training sessions and supplies were provided by the museum at no cost to the educators or to the District.

It Works!

Since being introduced to Savannah Chatham County Public Schools, the "Character Counts! Program" has been embraced with enthusiasm and excitement. Savannah area schools have seen major improvement in the behavior of their students in the classroom and community, thanks to the support of the Mighty Eighth Museum.

The program has support throughout the leadership of the school district. Superintendent Thomas Lockamy says "We're having to pay more attention to the social and emotional needs of children than ever before... If we don't, we're going to lose them." Pupil Personnel Director Quintina Miller-Fields graduated from Savannah High School and spent twelve years in the Army, attaining the rank of Captain. Dr Miller-Fields is a no nonsense person. She has a perfect background for her position and she runs the "Character Counts!" program. Principals and teachers both agree that emphasis on character is a critical need among students of all ages.

Kim Newman, principal of Thunderbolt Elementary and desperate to create a pro-active response to the alarming number of discipline referrals she was receiving, agreed to be the test school—the first to implement the "Character Counts!" program in 2010.

Mrs. Newman quickly saw a dramatic change in her students (and staff!). Behavioral problems declined markedly, going from 80-plus discipline referrals in the 2009 – 2010 school year to less than five in 2010 – 2011. She attributes this improvement in behavior directly to the "Character Counts !" program.

A year ago on Veteran's day, Kim asked me to speak to the entire student body. There were 420 school children from kindergarten through fifth grade all sitting on the gym floor, and not one child was out of order or even said a word. The gym had signs hanging down with the six pillars on them and quotations from famous statesmen such as Winston Churchill: "Never give in." It was very impressive.

Clearly, students are getting the message. They are seeing that little things add up to big things. In an effort to target at-risk youth, the Mighty Eighth, in collaboration with the Savannah Chatham County Public School System began hosting "Super Saturdays" in January 2012.These monthly seminars focus on either elementary, middle, or high school students. They expand upon the importance of good character, good decision making, and how students can make their homes, schools, and community, better places with simple actions.

Students may be referred by their high school guidance counselor, or a parent/guardian who must attend the seminar with them. After the seminar, students and parents enjoy a free lunch and a free tour of the museum where they hear stories of character during World War II directly from the veterans who were there.

To recognize that good character does not simply mean good grades, the Mighty Eighth has recently partnered with WTOC, a local CBS affiliate, to sponsor a "Character Counts! Student of the Month." Students will be nominated by their principals for displaying excellent character. One student will be chosen from the nominees and featured in a news piece on WTOC, and in a display at the Museum, which will describe why the student was chosen.

Future Plans

The key to success for the "Character Counts!" program is consistency. The Museum will continue to train new teachers, and offer refresher courses for those who have already been trained. A conference was held in September, 2012 at the Mighty Eighth, where teachers, staff and other adults who work with community youth learned new ideas to help students understand the importance of good character in life.

This is not a one year fix. While there already have been dramatic changes within the schools and community, students and teachers must continue this dialogue until it becomes engrained in them. It's a commitment to work together to make Savannah's community, from children to adults, among the best in the nation, so that future generations will continue to show the amazing character of the Greatest Generation.

What It Has Meant To Me

The Museum has been a wonderful experience for me. I have met tens of thousands of great people from all over the world and my message has been well received by young and old. I've had a chance to give that message to my children, grandchildren, and great grandchildren. When I take people on tours, I can relate to them as if they were my own family.

Deep in my heart, I feel I have been spared these many years by the good Lord, who has given me a very large responsibility: to pass the torch on to this new generation by honoring those who paid the ultimate sacrifice, giving their lives for our great country and our freedom. I also want to pay homage to those survivors who laid their lives on the line for the same reason with total disregard for the consequences.

Finally, I hope that I have left a lasting memory of my life-long friends and their families here at the National Museum of the Mighty Eighth Air Force: Walt Hays, Bob Haldane, Don Haldane, Don McCullough, Ed and Harry Van Tassel, and of course our mentor, "Pop" Dolan: We had some great times to look back on. They won and lost a few games, but in the game of life they were winners.

In Flanders Fields

By: Lieutenant Colonel John McCrae, MD (1872-1918)

"In Flanders Fields the poppies blow

Between the crosses row on row,

That mark our place; and in the sky

The larks, still bravely singing, fly

Scarce heard amid the guns below.

We are the dead. Short days ago

We lived, felt dawn, saw sunset glow,

Loved and were loved, and now we lie

In Flanders fields

Take up our quarrel with the foe:

To you from failing hands we throw

The torch; be yours to hold it high.

If ye break with us who die

We shall not sleep, though poppies grow

In Flanders fields"

Paul Grassey has authored articles
in several veteran's periodicals,
has appeared on local and national television,
and regularly presents to audiences
on veteran's issues and character development.

To purchase personalized copies of

It's Character
That Counts

You may contact the author directly at
characterpcg@aol.com

Discounts are available
for orders of 10 or more